The ultimate party book for kids

All You Need to Make Your Kid's Party a Hit!

Samuel Rice and Cissy Azar

Contents

Introduction

Children love a party. It's a fabulous way to celebrate an occasion, share the day with friends, wear a favourite outfit, play riotous games and to have fun. Planning a children's party can be a time-consuming activity and with so many things to organise, order and find, it's enough to send stress levels soaring. Yet parties should be fun and exciting, so hosting one can be a pleasure.

The Ultimate Party Book for Kids shows you how, with thought, careful planning and plenty of organisation, you can create a memorable and fun-filled party environment for all your guests. From innovative decorations to fabulous food ideas that children will love to eat, we'll guide you through every step of the way so there's really no need to break the budget or feel overwhelmed by parental playground pressure. We include plenty of helpful tips to make your party a success, and there are gentle reminders throughout to ensure that all the boxes are ticked and nothing is forgotten.

We've arranged all the information that you need to consider in a logical order and followed this with a host of party ideas organised according to the most popular themes that children just adore. Each theme has been specially designed to appeal to a range of ages and a mix of boys and girls. Within each you'll find a selection of recipes for the children as well as their parents, along with ideas for decorating the party area and some first-rate party games guaranteed to engender good will and lots of laughter among your guests. Some games are essential for every party no matter what the theme and we show you how to taper each to match the theme.

Planning the Perfect Party

Successful parties begin with being organised, and the sooner you start planning the more chance you have of sourcing everything that you need within budget. Start by creating a list of all the things that need doing. Organise your list into order of importance and work your way through it methodically; there's no point sending out invitations until you have the date, venue and entertainment (if appropriate) confirmed. Below is a sample list that you may find helpful.

1 Pick the party date and time, but have a few other dates in mind just in case.

2 Choose a location and if it's not going to be at home, check its availability with your date choices.

3 Choose a theme.

4 Decide if you're going to hire an entertainer. Sourcing entertainers is easy enough on the internet, though recommendation from other satisfied parents can also be a great way to find one. If using a venue and entertainment, make sure that both are available on the required date before booking either.

5 Book the venue. Some locations, such as halls and community centres, book up a long time in advance.

6 Book entertainment, if you've chosen not to organise games yourself.

7 Decide who to invite

8 Send out invitations—you could link these to your theme.

9 Organise and order a cake, if you're not making it yourself.

10 Choose your decorations, source and order them.

11 Decide what food you'll be supplying. If you need a trial run-through of different or new recipes arrange to do this ahead of the schedule. Write a shopping list for absolutely everything you need.

12 Organise party bags.

13 Buy some 'thank you' cards to send out once the party is over.

By creating a list you'll find it easy to track your progress. It will also give your planning focus and help you establish a realistic timescale to work to. Getting organised helps to eliminate the possibility of forgetting an important element, such as a birthday cake that might cause chaos were it to be forgotten.

CHOOSING A DATE AND TIME

Check
- The date of the birthday
- Is it in a school holiday?
- Is it on a public holiday?
- Will your friends and family be available?
- Are there any potential date clashes?

Check
- Children's age
- Nap times
- Weekend hobbies
- Mealtime party or snack-time party

Check the school calendar as well as the public holiday calendar to see if the birthday date falls on a school day, weekend or school holiday. Friends that your child might like to invite may be away in the school holidays and your child might be very upset if their best friend is unable to attend because they are away on holiday. Check with your family and friends to make sure that they are available on the chosen date either to help out as well as to attend the party. The last thing you want is to put heart and soul into organising a party only to have to cancel it because another event takes precedence.

Once you've selected a couple of potential dates, decide what time the party will start and how long it will go on. If the children are very young, they may have a nap schedule to keep to and if this is broken you could find yourself with some very unhappy guests, or you could factor it in to your planning. If the children are older then you'll have more flexibility. Children often take part in weekend activities and may not be able to attend if the party time clashes with their other commitments. Ultimately you'll have to decide what the priority is—choosing the date and time that's most convenient, or hosting the party with one or two of your child's preferred friends unable to attend.

Children's parties traditionally include a food break. If you choose to hold a party over a mealtime then you'll be providing a meal for the guests. However, if you choose to have your party in the early afternoon or mid-morning only a snack may be required.

CHOOSING A VENUE

When considering your choice of venue you might start by thinking about the season in which the party will be held. If you have a winter date, it makes sense to choose an indoor venue where rain and cold weather will not hinder the party. If you are having the party in the summer months then you may consider having the party outside.

Consider how many children you would like to invite to the party. If you are thinking about having the party at home, will there be enough space to accommodate everyone? If not, think about using other potential venues such as church and community halls, scout huts, parks or beaches, for example.

The location needs to be appropriate for the party's theme. A mini olympics party, for example, will need an appropriate amount of space in which the games and activities can be played. Don't forget to factor in the helpers too—they all take up space and need accommodating.

If you decide to hire a venue, make sure that you book early as many book out quickly. You'll not be the only one planning a party!

Check
- Season (potential weather conditions)
- Inside or outside
- Number of children you are planning to invite
- Type / theme of party
- Venue availability

CHOOSING A THEME

Check

- Ask your child what they would like
- Choose a theme that you can cater for
- Consider all the children attending the party
- Choose an age-appropriate theme

Some children will have a very clear idea about the type of party that they would like to have. Include your child in the discussion and decision-making to ensure you're all working towards the same goal. There are so many great characters and themes to choose from, and though you may think you know what your child would love, it might be a theme that he or she has grown out of. Having said that, you can always help the decision-making along by making suggestions and steering towards a theme that you think you'll be able to cater for, as well as one you know they'll enjoy.

While the party is for your child, it's also about providing enjoyment and entertainment for all their guests, so if you're inviting boys and girls, choose a theme that can be tailored to suit both. Finally, make sure that the theme is appropriate for the age of the child. Some themes might scare young children, for example those that include characters wearing masks, while others might appear childish to older children

Once you've chosen a theme, stick with it! Changing your mind halfway through planning can lead to unnecessary stress as well as mistakes. You don't want to find that that perfect birthday cake you ordered arrives and is actually for the wrong theme!

CHOOSING ENTERTAINMENT

Entertainment is an essential element of every party. While very young children will be happy to play with toys, having a large number of children arrive at your home or choice of venue can be daunting if you haven't organised how to entertain them. You don't want the kids to arrive and there be nothing for them to do, or they may quickly become bored and cause havoc.

There are two choices: You can either organise some games and activities for the children, or if the idea of keeping all your child's friends occupied fills you with dread, you could hire an entertainer.

The children will need entertaining for at least half of the party time, so if you decide to organise your own games and activities you'll need to do plenty of advance preparation. Also you'll be juggling several duties at the same time so having a small army of helpers to prepare food and greet guests will assist towards the smooth running of your party.

Hiring an Entertainer

A trained, experienced and professional entertainer can add a delightful dimension to a party, removing a whole organisational layer from your to-do checklist and providing you with some rest and breathing space. Entertainers may tell stories, introduce familiar characters, organise singing and dancing, present a mime show, play games, provide a puppet show or present a whole host of other imaginative ideas to keep children entertained. Once you've found a prospective company, make sure that it can supply the character/theme you are looking for and that it will be available at the time of your party. Ensure that any games and activities are appropriate for the party / venue, and that you are happy with the program that will be delivered.

Check

- Booking a reputable company is essential. Speak to other parents and friends for recommendations.
- Search the internet for different types of entertainers.
- Always read the testimonials and check when they were written.
- Ensure that the entertainers have been police-checked and that the company has insurance. This is also important from a safety perspective.
- Check that it can supply the character / theme you are looking for.
- Make sure you are happy with the games and activities included.theme

INVITATIONS AND PARTY ETIQUETTE

Check

- Send out the invitations well ahead of the party.
- Decide who you are inviting.
- Decide upon an appropriate time to hand out the invitations.theme

Send out invitations several weeks in advance of the party to ensure that everyone can place it in their diary.

Kids' parties have become big deals in today's playgrounds, and not just for the children. Yet, it's important not to feel pressured into holding a large and elaborate event simply because someone else in your child's class has. Each child wants different things for their special day. You're not obliged to invite the entire class just because your child has been invited to lots of parties.

However, there is a level of etiquette to be followed. If you're inviting the whole class, then sending your child to school with the invitations to be handed out makes life easy. If you've chosen instead to invite a select few, it would be more appropriate to hand out the invitations out of school hours or even to post them. This will stop other children from feeling excluded and help avoid awkwardness at the school gates with the other mums whose kids are not invited.

MANAGING YOUR CHILD'S EXPECTATIONS

As the party date approaches, your child will undoubtedly begin to feel excited. Deciding who to invite, writing the invitations and handing them out all add to the sense of occasion, so it's important to prepare your child on what you consider to be appropriate behaviour for the party and what your expectations are. Sometimes children forget how to behave when they are overwhelmed with excitement. Explaining how to behave during the entertainment will help make the party enjoyable for all the children.

Having lots of people present can also be daunting, so it's important to run through who will be present and what will happen and when so that they don't become frightened or timid on the day.

When your guests arrive the host child should greet them politely. If guests have brought presents, explain how to take the gift gently (rather than snatch), to thank the giver for their generosity, and to put the gift in a pre-selected place to be opened later.

If you have booked an entertainer, prepare your child so that they know that a special guest will be coming to run the games and activities. This is especially important if your child is nervous with strangers.

At the end of the party, have the birthday child thank each guest for attending.

Points to discuss
- There will be a lot of people at the party.
- How to greet the guests nicely.
- If given a present, how to receive the present and say thank you.
- If hiring an entertainer, prepare your child for the special guest.
- Explain what behaviour is expected throughout the party.
- Remember to thank the guests for attending at the end of the party.

HEALTH & SAFETY

Now you are well on your way to planning the ultimate kids party. The date has been chosen, the invitations are out and you've begun to plan the yummy food for the guests.

Food

It is always important to remember that some children have allergies. While planning what yummy things you will be serving to your guests, you should also check if anyone has any allergies. Avoiding common ingredients associated with allergies, such as nuts, can help. An easy way to find out if any of your child's friends have allergies will be to ask your child's school teacher, as they will most likely have common knowledge of any allergies the children in the class might have. You can also contact the parents, or even include a note on the invite asking parents to let you know of any allergies.

Don't serve food straight from the oven because it may be too hot. Serve food with napkins to make sure children don't burn themselves.

Make sure there is an adult to supervise the food table and ensure children don't choke if they eat in a hurry. Keep someone on hand to mop up spills and to keep flies or pets away from the food.

Activities

It's party time and everyone wants to have a great time. And to ensure that everyone has a fantastic time, you should always make sure that the games and activities you have planned for the party are age-appropriate, as well as child-safe. This could include using child-sized utensils such as scissors and glue for any arts and crafts activities.

If you have decided to use an entertainer, make sure that they have planned an age-appropriate program for the children, as well as advising them on the type of space they will be working in so they are able to avoid any potential dangers.

Finally, make sure that before the party you have cleared away any toys and other bits and pieces that may cause a tripping hazard while the children are playing.

Keeping it safe

- Play age-appropriate games and activities.
- Use child-safe utensils.
- Plan activities appropriate for the space you are using.
- Clear away any tripping hazards.
- Supervise all the time. Never leave young children unattended.

PARTY THEMES

Not everyone has hours to spend dreaming up ideas for a party. So to make your job a little easier, we've put plenty of great ideas together for you. We've included some creative suggestions for fabulous decorations, appetising recipes, and we've listed games and activities to entertain your guests that are specific to a party theme.

PARTY BAGS

Party bags are always a big hit at children's parties. They are usually given out at the end of the party as something the children can take home with them. You can fill them with all sorts of goodies; they are sure to add that finishing touch to your child's party.

Ideas for party bag fillers:

Pirate
- Pirate patches
- Telescope
- Gold chocolate coins
- Spade (to dig for treasure)

Princess
- Tiara
- Nail varnish
- Small comb or brush
- Candy necklace

Superhero
- Superhero mask
- Cape
- Stickers
- Small water gun

Fairy
- Wand
- Glitter
- Small fairy wings
- Cupcakes

Jungle
- Nets
- Kids' binoculars
- Toy butterflies
- Camouflage face paint

Witch or Wizard
- Wand
- Spell note book
- Witch/wizard hat
- Toy spiders

Clown
- Red nose
- Water spraying flower
- Clown tie
- Fuzzy wig

Under the Sea/Mermaid
- Jelly (fish) sweets and lollies
- Bubbles
- Seashell necklace
- Grow your own spider monkeys

AFTER THE PARTY

Once the party has finished, have some calming activities ready so that the birthday child doesn't have a party 'crash'. It's likely that he or she will have received plenty of presents so let them play with their new toys. If they're too noisy and will exacerbate an already hyped-up and overexcited child, then have some DVDs at hand that they can watch while you clear up/relax.

Don't forget to send out thank you cards to all your guests. It might seem old fashioned but it's still the easiest and politest way to thank your guests for attending the party as well as for any gift they gave.

Treas

Pirate Parties

Pirate parties are fantastic for boys and girls, and can work for a whole range of ages from one to 10. If you are inviting lots of children to the party where their ages and genders will vary, this is the perfect option to ensure that everyone has a wonderful time. When you organise the activities for the children you can weave a story with them to help set the tone and build the excitement.

Decorations

The internet is a fabulous source of suppliers for inexpensive party decorations. All you need are a few ideas. Decorate your space with pirate flags, inflatable palm trees and black and gold balloons to create a fun pirate feel. Source some small treasure chests in which to place sweets for the party and have a larger chest that you fill with eye patches and swords for the kids to collect when they arrive. Small plastic or chocolate coins are sure to appeal to everyone and can be scattered throughout the room.

Variation: Use black pirate flags as tablecloths or use black sheets of paper or card on the table along with chalk and allow the kids to create their own pirate flag tablecloth. Not only will this add to the party decorations, it will also be a fun activity. Make sure that you have plenty of paper and chalk so the kids can have several turns to perfect their masterpieces.

Check

- Use small treasure chests to hold sweets.
- Fill a large treasure chest with eye patches and swords for the guests.
- Blow up (or real if you want to update your garden) palm trees.
- Placing pirate flags throughout the room.
- Black and gold balloons.
- Pirate flags for tablecloths, or black sheets of paper that the kids can decorate with their own pirate flags using chalk.

Hint...

Less is more. Don't go 'overboard' with too many decorations.

Activities

1 Create a Pirate Flag

This is a fun arts and crafts activity where the children can let their imaginations run wild. They'll also have their own pirate flag to take home.

You will need:

black card or paper
chalk
wooden skewers
glue/sticky tape

Invite the children to sit at a table or on the floor and give each a sheet of black paper and a piece of chalk—protect the work surface, if necessary. Tell the children a story and explain that 'while you were on an island looking for treasure someone came aboard the pirate ship and stole the pirate flag. We can't sail without a pirate flag! Who would like to help create a new pirate flag for the ship?'.

Hint...

Have extra paper if the children want to create more than one flag.

Once the children have decorated their flags, glue or stick a wooden skewer to the back so that the children can wave their flags.

Alternatively, ask the children to design one large pirate flag together using a large piece of black paper or cardboard. Once they've completed the flag, hang it on the wall for the party.

2 Treasure Hunt

What do pirates love? TREASURE! This fun activity will take the kids on a wonderful adventure and have them searching high and low for the hoard.

You will need:

gold or silver chocolate coins
a treasure map (optional)
small treasure chests
riddles or clues

This one needs plenty of space. For very young children you could make a pirate map of the area where the treasure is hidden and mark the treasure sites with a cross on the map so that all they have to do is work their way around the different sites—you could lead very young children around the venue using the map and encouraging them to look for the treasure. You can also give them a small treasure chest each that they can collect their treasure in. For older children you may decide to give them cryptic clues as to where to search for the treasure.

Make sure they have a point of reference to work from and that the treasure is accessible. Older children will need a greater challenge, otherwise they may just walk around the space looking for chocolate coins and the game could fall flat and be over very quickly. Giving children a chain of clues that they have to solve, while at the same time telling a story, will make the children work together as a team. Clue 1 directs the children to a site that contains hidden clue 2. The site of clue 2 contains clue 3 and so on. Make it as hard or as easy as befits the age of the children involved.

To organise in advance

- Before the party and while your child is not around, hide the chocolate coins around the party venue, out of plain sight.
- To create a treasure map draw the area of the treasure hunt on an A4 sheet of paper – it doesn't need to be to scale. Mark the hidden treasure on the map using a cross. To give the map an aged appearance, paint it with a cold wet teabag and leave to dry. Cut, shred or burn the edges of the paper to give a distressed finish.

3 Captain's Corner

A game of orientation and memory

You will need:

plenty of space

Allocate names to four different points within the room. One wall may be port, and opposite may be starboard, for example. Each point of the room is associated with a designated action that the children must perform when they arrive there. For example,

For port, the kids say 'aye aye captain' and salute.

At starboard, the children shout, 'land ahoy'.

At ship's wheel, the kids must steer the ship.

At ship's rigging, the children mime climbing the rigging.

At Captain's sleeping quarters the children must pretend to be asleep, making snoring noises.

With the places and actions decided, take the children on a tour of the space, stopping at each and providing a short, yet exciting story to do with it and explaining / showing the children the action that must be performed there.

When the children are familiar with each place and action, you can begin the game. Call out different places for the children to run to and perform the action that is associated with that location. You can repeat this several times using different points in the room and varying the speed. As the children become more familiar with where each place is, you may also choose to show the action rather than call out the place name so that the children must remember which action goes with which place. You can then even swap the places and actions around so the children have to perform a different action at each place.

4 Fan the Fish

This is a game for two or more teams and for which you need plenty of space.

You will need:

a fish shape cut from lightweight paper—one for each player

a folded newspaper—one for each player

The children in each team stand one behind the other in a queue. The first player puts their fish on the floor on the start line. The child flaps the newspaper up and down in a fanning action in order to create a draught. The draught makes the fish move. The aim is to move the fish on an air current created by the newspaper from the start point at one side of the room to the finish point at the other. As soon as the first child crosses the finish line, the second child starts. The first team home wins. If the fish are cut out of very lightweight paper they float all over-creating mayhem and hilarity as the children dash behind them to move them.

Demonstrate the game first and then let each child have a go to be sure they've understood what to do before the game proper begins.

5 Pass the Cannonball

This is a hands-free team game of skill and dexterity, in which children pass an object from one player to the next without using their hands.

You will need:

large oranges, semi-inflated balloons or ball-pit soft balls

The children stand in a line with the first two team members facing each other. Player one holds a large orange under his or her chin then stands with his hands behind his back. Player 1 has to pass the orange to player 2 without either of them using their hands. The skill is in being able to pass and collect the orange from one player to the next using only the neck and chin. Player 2 turns to player 3 and repeats the exercise. The first team to pass the orange along the line of team members wins. If a player drops the orange, he or she may use his hands to restore it to beneath his chin.

6 Disarm the Cannonball

A team game to play outside in the summer with bare feet.

You will need:

semi-inflated balloons filled with water and tied with string

Tie a water-filled balloon to each player's ankle. The aim of the game is to burst the balloons of the opposing team member. Use different colour balloons for each team to make it easy for players to identify their opponents, if you like. The team to retain any filled balloons wins.

7 X Marks the Spot

A variation on the childhood classic 'Pin the tail on the donkey'.

You will need:

a pirate map marked with a large cross.
a sticker for each child, with their name written on it
a blindfold

Pin the map to the wall at the children's shoulder height. Ask the first child to stand in front of the map and locate the cross. Give the child the sticker with their name on it. Put the blindfold on the child and turn him or her on the spot three or four times—the aim is to be slightly dizzy and disoriented. Ask the child to stick the sticker where he thinks the cross is. The child whose sticker is nearest the cross is the winner.

Pirate Cake

Chocolate Cake

Serves 15-25

375 g (13 oz) butter

300 g (10½ oz) compound milk
chocolate

45 g (1½ oz) Dutch (dark,
unsweetened) cocoa powder

225 g (8 oz) self-raising (self-rising)
flour

115 g (4 oz) plain (all-purpose) flour

310 g (11 oz) caster (superfine)
sugar

120 ml (4 fl oz) buttermilk

15 ml (1 tablespoon) vanilla extract

4 large eggs, lightly beaten

2 quantities Chocolate Ganache, plus
extra for decoration (see Basic
Recipes)

1 kg (36 oz) white fondant icing, for
decorating

edible food colouring—blue, brown

The fondant topping can be done
two days in advance.

Preheat oven to 160°C/325°F/Gas mark 3. Lightly grease and line two 24cm-wide (9¾in) cake pans.

Melt the butter and the chocolate together in a double boiler, or in a large heatproof bowl set over a pan of gently simmering water. Stir the cocoa powder into the chocolate mixture. Remove from the heat.

Sift the flours into a bowl, add the sugar, then mix in the buttermilk, vanilla and eggs. Add the chocolate mixture and mix until combined.

Split the batter between the 2 prepared cake tins and bake for 75–85 minutes or until a skewer inserted into the centre comes out clean. Leave to cool in the tin for 10 minutes, then turn out on to a wire rack.

Once cooled, spread a thin layer of ganache on top of one cake, then stack the other on top. Cover all over with ganache, leaving a little for decorating. Refrigerate to set.

To make the decoration, colour about 250-300g (9–10½oz) fondant icing blue. On a clean bench dusted with icing sugar, roll out the blue fondant into a 10mm (⅓in) sheet. (You can also roll out straight onto wax paper, this may be a little easier.) Using the cake tin, trace out a circle and carefully cut a circle. Using the rolling pin, carefully wrap the circle onto the rolling pin and gently lift onto a wax paper-lined tray. Colour about 150-200g (5–7oz) fondant brown.

Now roll out a piece of brown fondant as above, and again use the cake tin to trace another circle. Just above halfway up the circle, cut a crescent-moon shape for the boat's hull. Use a sharp knife to gently score lines for the planks on the hull. Use the rolling pin again to lift the hull onto the blue fondant, lining up the bottoms.

Using the off cuts of the brown fondant, roll out a long piece of brown fondant to make the 'gunwale' or railing. Place this where the brown and blue meet and shape it to the curve you've cut. Leave a little on either side for a bow and stern.

Use some ganache, gently melted in low microwave, in a piping bag to draw the masts, cannon ports and ship's wheel, allow to dry before adding the masts.

Using some remaining white fondant, cut some triangles for sails and a mast flag, curve them slightly for a wind-filled look and stick in place them against the masts, using a little water to affix them.

Allow to set for 24–48 hours or until fully hardened before carefully placing it on top of the cake. If you are confident and have worked with fondant before, you can work straight onto the cake. You need only a few hours to set the fondant.

Decorate around the base with chocolate coin confectionery.

Weigh Anchor

Pirate Ship Calzone

Makes 2-3 ships serves 8-12

CALZONE DOUGH

250 ml (9 fl oz) lukewarm water

½ teaspoon sugar

16 g (½ oz) active dry yeast

740 g (24 oz) bread/baker's flour

1 teaspoon salt

1 teaspoon olive oil

1 beaten egg, for brushing

1-2 sheets shortcrust pastry, about
   150-200 g (5-7oz) each

4-6 wooden skewers, sharp ends
   removed

FILLING

1 onion, diced

200 g (7 oz) ricotta cheese

80 g (2½ oz) fetta cheese

100g (3½ oz) diced ham

50 g (1¾ oz) breadcrumbs

2 eggs + 1 egg, beaten, for brushing

50 g (1¾ oz) mozzarella cheese

OTHER IDEAS

Serve watermelon and rockmelon in balls as 'cannonballs'.
Make sandwiches, cut into triangles and place one triangle standing up as little pirate ships.

Preheat the oven to 180°C/350°F/Gas mark 4. To make the dough, place the water and sugar in a bowl and sprinkle with the yeast. Cover with a tea towel and leave for 5 minutes until foamy. Sift in the flour and salt and mix together until a dough forms. Knead for a few minutes. Grease a large bowl with the olive oil. Place the dough in the bowl, cover with a clean kitchen towel and leave in a warm place for 1 hour until doubled in size. Now remove the dough and knead until the dough shrinks back to its original size. Divide the dough into 2 and leave, covered, for another 30 minutes.

Lay the dough out and by gently stretching (don't use a rolling pin) form two ovals. Make a slit at each end and twist the ends together to form the 'bow' and 'stern'. Drape the dough into a greased oval heatproof dish. Brush the edges with a little egg.

To make the filling, place all the ingredients into a bowl and mix well. Stuff the 'ships' and bake in the same oven for 20–30 minutes until dough is golden.

To make the sails, soak the skewers in water for 1 hour then dry for 5 minutes. Cut two triangles from the shortcrust pastry. Drape the pastry over a heatproof cylinder like a glass jar or log pan. Brush with egg and cook for 10 minutes. Remove and poke the skewers through the sails. Cook for a further 5 minutes.
You can also use paper or muslin cloth to make the sails.

Pirates' Bounty

Chocolate Doubloons

Makes 10

2 tablespoons caster (superfine)
   sugar
1/3 cup double cream
280 g (10 oz) dark melting chocolate
edible gold dust or paint

Place the sugar in a dry, deep saucepan and cook on medium heat. The sugar will melt and turn a golden colour.

Add the cream carefully; it will bubble and froth. Remove from the heat immediately. Place the chocolate in a heatproof bowl and add the hot cream/sugar mixture. Stir gently until the chocolate melts. Let cool for 15–20 minutes or until the mixture starts to thicken. Using your hands, roll 10 balls. Now flatten the balls into disc shapes and place on waxed paper to set. These can be done up to 2 days prior and stored in the fridge. Before serving, paint or spray with edible gold dust.

Serve the gold coins with pearls (yoghurt-coated raisins).

Chocolate Cupcakes

Makes 18

120g (4 oz) milk compound
   chocolate
30g (1 oz) dark cocoa powder
250 ml (9 fl oz) water
125 g soft unsalted butter
1¼ cups muscovado sugar
3 large eggs
250g (9 oz) self-raising (self-rising)
   flour
80 g (2½ oz) plain (all-purpose)
   flour

FROSTING
300 g (10½ oz) dark chocolate
300 g (10½ oz) sour cream

Preheat oven to 160°C/325°F/Gas mark 3. Lightly grease an 18-hole cupcake tin and line with paper cases.

Place 120g (4oz) milk chocolate, cocoa and the water in a heatproof bowl and melt over a double boiler. Cream the butter and the sugar with electric beaters on high until light and fluffy. Reduce to a medium speed and add the eggs slowly one at a time.

Fold through the chocolate mixture with a metal spoon, then sift in the flours and fold through until completely mixed.

Spoon the mixture into the paper cases, place in oven and bake for 20 minutes or until when pressed gently the cupcakes spring back.

For the frosting, melt the dark chocolate over a double boiler or in the microwave on medium. Allow to cool to room temperature. Whip the sour cream with electric beaters; add the chocolate gradually until incorporated. Top each cupcake with some frosting.

Mini Hotdogs

Makes 18

500 g (17½ oz) puff pastry
18 mini cocktail hotdogs/frankfurters
1 egg, beaten

Preheat oven to 180°C/350°F/Gas mark 4. Line 2 baking trays with non-stick paper.

Cut 18 squares of pastry 3 x 3cm (1 x 1in). Place a hotdog on top of each square, diagonally across. Fold one corner over the hotdog then fold the other corner, so the hotdog is completely wrapped in pastry with the ends of the hotdog still visible.

Place onto trays leaving a little space between each. Brush with a little egg, and bake for 20 minutes or until golden. Allow to cool slightly before serving.

Mini Pizzas

Makes 12

6 English muffins, halved

2 tablespoons olive oil

½ cup pizza sauce (see Whale Tail recipe)

1 cup grated mozzarella or pizza cheese

50 g (1¾ oz) pepperoni or ham, diced

Preheat oven to 190°C/375°F/Gas mark 5. Line 2 baking trays with non-stick paper.

Place each muffin half onto baking trays, cut side up. Brush each with a little olive oil. Spread a teaspoon of pizza sauce over the tops of each muffin half. Sprinkle each with cheese, then pepperoni or ham.

Bake for 10 minutes or until cheese is melted. Allow to cool slightly before serving.

Treasure Top Cupcakes

Makes 12

150 g (5 oz) butter, at room
    temperature
1 cup caster (superfine) sugar
3 eggs
1 teaspoon vanilla extract
½ cup milk
1½ cups self-raising (self-rising) flour,
    sifted
500 g (17 oz) fondant
blue icing paste
yellow icing paste
icing (confectioners') sugar
royal icing (see Basic Recipes)

DECORATIONS
12 chocolate gold coins
blue edible glitter
12 plastic palm trees
12 skull and crossbones flags

Preheat oven to 160°C/325°F/Gas mark 3 and line a 12-cup muffin tray with cupcake papers.

Cream butter and sugar together until light and fluffy. Add eggs one at a time, beating well after each addition. Add the vanilla.

Add half the milk and half the flour, mix, then add the remaining milk and flour. Divide the mixture evenly between the paper cases.

Bake for 20 minutes until cooked. Cool for 5 minutes, then turn onto a cooling rack.

Colour 300g (10½oz) of the fondant blue, and 200g (7oz) yellow. Spread a small amount of royal icing on top of each cupcake—this will secure the fondant.

On a surface dusted with icing sugar, roll out blue fondant to 5mm (⅛in) thick. Using a round cutter, cut 12 circles from the fondant. Roll out yellow fondant and cut out circles, then cut and discard crescents from the circles. Use royal icing to attach the yellow and blue fondant, then place each on top of a cupcake. Attach the decorations to make each cupcake a desert island.

Rocky Road

Serves 10-20

400 g (14 oz) good-quality milk
   compound chocolate, broken into
   pieces
125 g (4 oz) marshmallows, chopped
   roughly
100 g (3½ oz) Turkish delight,
   chopped roughly
50 g (1¾ oz) glacé cherries, roughly
   chopped
¼ cup shredded coconut
100 g (3½ oz) plain milk coffee
   biscuits, roughly chopped

Line a 3cm (1in) deep, 16 x 25cm (6¼ x 9¾in)
slab pan with wax paper, allowing the edges to
over hang.

Melt the chocolate over a double boiler,
stirring until smooth. Toss in all other
ingredients and combine. Press the mixture into
the lined pan evenly. Refrigerate for 3 hours or
until set.

Turn out by grabbing the over-hanging edges
and ease out the slab. Cut into pieces and serve.

Volcano Island

Makes 1

6 x 340 g (12 oz) packets butter
   cake mix
2 quantity Buttercream Frosting (see
   Basic Recipes)
green icing paste
red icing paste
orange icing paste
½ cup desiccated coconut
1 quantity chocolate Buttercream
   Frosting (see Basic Recipes)
¼ cup drinking chocolate powder
   (Milo)

DECORATIONS

2 red sour straps
milk chocolate TV mix
3 plastic palm trees
4 plastic lizards

Preheat oven to 180°C/ 350°F/Gas mark 4 and butter and line the cake tins.

Prepare 2 packets of cake mix, following directions on packet, and pour into a pudding basin tin 19.5cm (7¾in) in diametre, 5.5cm (2in) deep. Prepare remaining 4 packets of cake mix and pour into a rectangular tin, 27.5 x 22.5cm (10¾ x 8¾in). Bake for 30 minutes, cover with foil and bake for another 30 minutes. Remove the pudding basin cake and bake the rectangular cake for a further 15 minutes. Test with a skewer to make sure the cakes are cooked. Leave to cool for 10 minutes, then turn onto a cooling rack.

While cakes cool, colour half the butter cream frosting green. Divide the remaining butter cream frosting in half again, colour half red and half orange. Place the coconut in either a bowl or plastic bag and mix through green paste, a little at a time, to achieve desired colour.

Use a serrated knife to level the cakes. Using a palette knife, frost the rectangular cake green, then sprinkle over the coconut. Frost the Dolly Varden cake with chocolate frosting and attach to the rectangular cake with skewers. Dust liberally with chocolate powder, then frost the top of the cake with red and orange icing.

Cut the sour straps into thin strips and attach to the top of volcano. Place the TV mix, palm tress and lizards on the rectangular cake.

Treasure Island

Makes 1

6 x 340 g (12 oz) packets butter
   cake mix
2 quantity Buttercream Frosting (see
   Basic Recipes)
blue icing paste
yellow icing paste

DECORATIONS

30 cm (11 3/4 in) piece liquorice strap
1 red sour strap
1 red jelly bean
blue and green rainbow chocolate
   chips
chocolate coins
3 plastic palm trees
1 skull and crossbones flag

Preheat oven to 180°C/350°F/Gas mark 4 and butter and line the cake tins.

Prepare 2 packets of cake mix, following directions on packet, and pour into a pudding basin tin 19.5cm (7¾in) in diametre, 5.5cm (2in) deep. Prepare remaining 4 packets of cake mix and pour into a rectangular tin, 27.5 x 22.5cm (10¾ x 8¾in). Bake for 30 minutes, cover with foil and bake for another 30 minutes. Remove the Dolly Varden cake and bake the rectangular cake for a further 15 minutes. Test with a skewer to make sure the cakes are cooked. Leave to cool for 10 minutes, then turn onto a cooling rack.

While cakes cool, colour half the butter cream frosting blue. Remove 2–3 tablespoons and colour dark blue. Colour remaining frosting yellow.

Use a serrated knife to level the cakes. Using a palette knife, frost the rectangular cake blue, then use the dark blue frosting to make waves. Frost the Dolly Varden cake yellow and attach to the rectangular cake with skewers.

Cut the liquorice strap to make shark fins. Use the sour strap and jelly bean to make the crab. Place the chocolate chips, coins, palm trees and flag on the cake.

X Marks the Spot

Lamb Cutlets with Parsley and Macadamia Rub

Serves 8-10

4-5 frenched lamb racks*
1 bunch parsley
½ bunch mint leaves
2 whole garlic cloves
50 g (1¾ oz) macadamia or
    Brazil nuts
20 g (⅔ oz) breadcrumbs
juice of 1 lemon
1 teaspoon olive oil
salt and pepper
mayonnaise or yoghurt

Preheat the oven to 200°C/ 400°F/Gas mark 6.

In a food processor, combine the parsley, mint, garlic, nuts, breadcrumbs, lemon juice and the olive oil. Whizz until you have a smooth paste. Set aside some of the mix for later. Rub a generous amount onto the racks (both side) and leave to marinate for 15 minutes.

Heat a tablespoon of oil in a large pan until medium hot. Brown each rack for 1 minute on each side. Place the racks into a baking dish and bake in the oven for 20 minutes (for medium rare). Rest the meat for 10 minutes.

Using a sharp, straight-edged knife, slice between each bone carefully to separate the cutlets. Arrange on a platter by criss-crossing the bones to make an X. Mix the leftover rub with a little mayonnaise or yoghurt and serve immediately.

*Frenched cutlets are easier to work with as the fat is already trimmed; however, if unavailable you can trim the fat yourself. Take a sharp knife and run it along the edges to separate the fat from the meat. Pull the fat off and use the knife to free the fat from the meat in sections, until all the fat comes off. Now cut the fatty parts from the bone for a 'frenched' finish.

Princess Parties

Princess Parties

A perfect dreamy theme for young girls. However, this doesn't mean that they are not appropriate if you have boys coming to the party too—simply make the party a princesses and knights party.

Ideal age group: 3–7 years

Decorations

There are plenty of princesses to choose from (Cinderella, Snow White, Aurora, Ariel, Jasmine, Rapunzel), so once you've decided on your heroine, stick with that so you can arrange a co-ordinating colour scheme to work with. For Cinderella, for instance, it would be appropriate to decorate in blue and white to match her costume. To decorate the table, pick tablecloths that match the princess's dress. You can also place co-ordinating flowers on the table in vases or 'crowns' that are the same colours as the princess's dress.

Placing bunches of helium balloons throughout the space is also a simple way to create a soft fairytale feel.

You could drape streamers from the outer edges of the room and have them all meet in the middle of the ceiling, creating a ballroom effect.

The more adventurous could place a picture frame (with no glass) in the room which the children could hold in front of themselves as if they are the portrait, and have their pictures taken.

Check
- Tablecloths in keeping with the princess's dress colour.
- Bouquets of flowers using the princess's colour scheme in vases or small crowns.
- Bunches of helium balloons throughout the room.
- Streamers hung around the room meeting in the middle to create a ballroom feel.
- Hanging picture frames (no glass) that the children can have their photos taken in.

Activities

If you have girls and boys at the party, then make sure the games are all-inclusive.

1 Create Your Own Crown/Decorate Your Own Shield

The children can let their imaginations run wild by creating their own princess crowns or designing their own knights' shields.

You will need:
A4 card (more than enough for each child)
crown stencil
shield stencil
sticky tape or glue
pair of scissors (to be used by a responsible adult only)
colouring pencils or pens

Pre-draw the outlines of crowns and shields on the A4 pieces of card, using the stencils. The crown stencils need to be large enough to fit around a child's head. Cut out each shape, ensuring there will be enough to go round and have a few spare. Cut strips of card 10cm (4in) long and 4cm (1¾in) wide and glue or tape the top and bottom part of a strip to the back of each cardboard shield to create a handle.

Remember...
Never leave children unattended with sharp items such as scissors.

As children arrive at the party, offer them a pre-cut shield or crown to colour in, then invite them to sit at a table that has been set up with colouring pencils and pens so that the children can begin their first activity.

Once the crowns are complete, stick the two ends of each crown together with glue or tape, testing for fit first.

2 Scare the Ugly Sisters

Those Ugly Sisters in Cinderella are so mean, it's time the princesses and knights got their own back. The kids will love playing this super sneaky trick.

You will need:

some Ugly Sisters (parents can volunteer)

space

Have the children line up side by side and facing you. Explain to them that they are about to practise sneaking up on the Ugly Sisters. But whenever the Ugly Sisters turn around and look at them, they must freeze like statues. If the Ugly Sisters catch them moving, they will make them go back to the beginning. Once the children are close enough to the Ugly Sisters they have to shout 'BOO' really loudly and scare the Ugly Sisters.

This game can be played over and over again, changing the way in which the children sneak up.

3 Musical Chairs

This is a fun classic game that the children will love playing.

You will need:

music and an adult to operate the sound

chairs, for all the children

Place all of the chairs in a circle, seats facing outwards. Make sure that each child has a chair. Play the music and at the same time the children proceed around the circle of chairs. When the music stops the children must find a chair to sit on. Do this several times until the children understand how to play the game.

Now remove one of the chairs from the circle as the music is playing and the children are walking around the chairs in a circle. Once the music stops, every child runs to find a chair to sit on. As there is one less chair than children, one child will be unable to find a chair and will be out. Remove a chair after each round until there is only one chair and two children circling it. The child to sit on the last chair when the music stops is the winner.

4 Musical Statues

A challenging game that can keep children entertained for ages.

You will need:

some music and someone to operate it
plenty of space

Children dance to the music but as soon as it stops they must turn to statues. Anyone who moves a muscle is out. The judge is at liberty to pull faces, tickle with a feather and attempt to make the children laugh. The last statue standing wins.

5 Find the Golden Slipper

A game of hide and seek.

You will need:

plenty of space with hiding places

Ask the children to stand in one room while you go off to hide a slipper. The more hiding places and the bigger the space the harder the game. The first person to find the slipper wins and is the next person to hide the slipper.

6 Retrieve the Castle Keys from the Dragon

The quieter you move the less chance you have of waking the sleeping dragon!

You will need:

a parent to play the dragon
a bunch of keys or other noisy object.

A blindfolded person sits in the centre of the room as the Dragon, guarding the keys to the castle at their feet. Each player takes a turn to approach the Dragon from a different angle and retrieve the keys, but if the dragon hears a noise and roars the player must sit down and the next player begins their attempt. In order to retrieve the keys the players must move silently. The player who wins returns the keys to their start point. If the Dragon hears all the players then the dragon wins.

Princess Birthday Cake

Red Velvet Cupcakes

Makes 18

725 g (1 lb 9 oz) plain (all-purpose)
  flour
20 g (²⁄₃ oz) Dutch (dark,
  unsweetened) cocoa powder
2.5 ml (½ teaspoon) salt
2.5 ml (½ teaspoon) baking powder
250 ml (9fl oz) buttermilk
5 ml (1 teaspoon) vanilla extract
30 ml (1 fl oz) red food colouring
120 g (4 oz) butter
300 g (10½ oz) granulated (white)
  sugar
2 large eggs, lightly beaten
5 ml (1 teaspoon) bicarbonate of
  soda (baking soda)
5 ml (1 teaspoon) white vinegar
1 quantity pink Buttercream Frosting
  for piping (see Basic Recipes)
#104 petal icing nozzle

Preheat the oven to 180°C/350°F/Gas mark 4.
Grease and line a 12-hole muffin pan with paper
cases.

Sift the flour, cocoa, salt and baking powder
into a large bowl.

In a separate bowl, mix the buttermilk, vanilla
and red colouring.

In an electric mixer, beat the butter with
the sugar until pale and creamy. Slowly add the
eggs, then scrape down the sides of the bowl.
Sift in one-third of the flour mixture and mix to
combine.

Slowly add half of the red buttermilk, then
another third of the flour mix, scraping down the
bowl between each addition. Add the rest of the
buttermilk, then the last of the flour and mix
until combined.

Red velvet's texture relies on a chemical
reaction between the bicarbonate of soda and
vinegar. Combine the two in a small bowl—the
mixture will bubble and froth. Stir into the cake
batter using a metal spoon. You must work
quickly here. Spoon the batter into the paper
cases and bake for 15–20 minutes or until a
skewer comes out clean when inserted into the
centre.

To make the roses, put a quantity of pink buttercream in a piping bag fitted with a #104 petal nozzle. Hold the cupcake at eye level in front of you. Hold the piping bag with the widest part of the nozzle at the bottom and the narrow side at the top. Keeping your hand holding the piping bag steady and turning the cupcake, pipe a semi-circle. Starting two-thirds of the way around the semi-circle, start another semi-circle. Continue to pipe partial circles starting a little before the last semi-circle finished. As you get to the outer petals, start twisting the piping bag slightly so the nozzle is more horizontal, in order to make the petal edges curl like a rose.

You can make the roses on wax paper and set aside to harden overnight, before placing them on the cupcakes, using a little buttercream (re-whipped) to 'glue' them on.

Wrap each cupcake in princess paper wrappers or cases. Place the cupcakes on a cupcake tower, or cake stand. You can decorate with a tiara on top, some pink tulle on the bottom, edible gems, sparklers or pink glitter.

For easier roses, use a star tip and swirl a snail shape onto the cupcakes.

Princess Pink Cupcakes

Makes 18

200 g (7 oz) soft unsalted butter
1¾ cups caster (superfine) sugar
2 teaspoons vanilla extract
1 tablespoon. pink food colouring
4 large eggs, at room temperature
2¾ cups self-raising (self-rising) flour
1 cup milk

FROSTING
160 g (5½ oz) unsalted butter
50 g (1¾ oz) sour cream
juice of one lemon
2 teaspoons milk
300 g (10½ oz) icing (confectioners')
   sugar
flower or pink star decorations

Preheat oven to 180°C/350°F/Gas mark 4. Line a muffin or cupcake pan with paper cases.

Place the butter and sugar in a clean bowl or stand mixer, and beat on high until light and fluffy. Turn down to a medium speed add the vanilla and pink colour. Add the eggs slowly, one at a time. Sift in the flour and fold in gently using a metal spoon. Fold in the milk.

Spoon the mixture into the paper cases.

Place in the oven for 15–20 minutes. When they are ready they should be golden brown, and when pressed gently on top, spring back.

Transfer to a wire rack to cool completely.

To make the frosting, place the butter, lemon and milk in a bowl and beat with electric mixer on high until pale and smooth. Gradually beat in the sour cream and all the sugar and beat for a further 3 minutes until smooth.

Use a spatula or a piping bag to apply the frosting. Attach the decorations.

Princess Pink Champagne

Pomegranate Lemonade

Serves 8-10

50 g (1¾ oz) caster (superfine)
    sugar
edible pink food colouring, gel or
    powder
lemonade
seeds of 1 pomegranate

Place some caster sugar into a zip lock bag. Use a toothpick (cocktail stick) to dab a drop of colour into the sugar.

Close the bag and shake until the sugar is a consistent colour. Use your fingers to rub the outside of the bag to loosen any colour blocks. If you use liquid colour you will have to dry the sugar for a few days.

Use the natural colouring of fresh pomegranate seeds to make a fun drink for mini princesses. Dip the rims of the glasses into a little water, shake off excess water, then dip into the pink sugar.

Pour some lemonade into glasses and add 6–8 pomegranate seeds. Serve immediately.

Strawberry Kiss

Strawberries in White Chocolate

Serves 12

250 g (9 oz) white chocolate
12 large strawberries
chocolate piping or pink icing
12 popsticks

Melt the chocolate in a double boiler until smooth.

Dip a little of the pop stick in the white chocolate and insert through the hull of the strawberry. Coat each strawberry in white chocolate, then place in a styrofoam block to hold the sticks upright while the chocolate sets.

Pipe 'rose' swirls over the coated strawberries using chocolate or pink icing.

OTHER IDEAS

Anything pink!
Add beetroot juice to hummus and serve with carrot and celery sticks for a fun dip.
Upside down ice cream cones dipped in pink icing for edible princess hats.
Make little crowns by topping round cookies with cream and cut strawberries around the outside.

The Princess & The Pea

Pea and Mint Flatbreads with Fetta and Roasted Red Peppers

Serves 12-20

1 cup (140 g/5 oz) cooked peas

1 onion

½ bunch mint

30 ml (2 tablespoons) water

225 g(8 oz/2 cups) plain (all-purpose) flour, plus extra for dusting

¼ teaspoon salt

1 teaspoon garam marsala

30-100 ml (1-3½ fl oz) ghee, clarified butter or oil for frying

100g (3½ oz) red bell peppers (capsicum), roasted and chopped (about 1-2 peppers)

¼ cup spring onions (scallions), chopped

100 g (3½ oz) fetta cheese, crumbled

1 lemon

100 g (3½ oz) smoked trout, flaked (optional)

To roast the peppers, put the red peppers on a lightly greased baking tray. Place them under a hot grill until the skin starts to char. Keep turning the peppers until the skin starts to wrinkle and come away from the flesh. Put the cooked peppers in a bowl and cover the bowl tightly with cling film, for about 1 hour. Peel away the skin. Tear in half and remove the stalk and seeds. Reserve the flesh. Roasted red peppers can be stored for a week or two in the refrigerator.

Place the peas, onion, mint and water in a food processor and blend to form a paste.

In a separate bowl, sift together the flour, salt and garam masala. Add the pea paste and mix until a dough forms (you may need to add a little more water). Allow the dough to rest for 30–40 minutes.

Roll out the dough into thin sheets (the thinner the better). Cut out circles 10–15cm (4–6in) diameter—use a saucer or side plate as a template. You may find it easier to roll small balls then roll each one out to a thin pancake.

Put ½ a teaspoon of ghee (enough to coat the bottom of the pan) into a small frying pan on medium-high heat. Once the oil is hot, fry each flatbread for about 2 minutes each side or until it starts to rise and bubble slightly, but still soft. Don't overcook them and let them get crispy.

In a separate bowl, mix the roasted red peppers, spring onions and crumbled fetta. Add a squeeze of lemon juice and toss together until well combined.

Form each flatbread into a cone shape and tie with a piece of cooking twine or string. Stuff each with some of the red pepper mixture and ocean trout, if using. Serve immediately.

* You will need to use an oil with a higher smoke point such as safflower, avocado, corn or peanut oil.

Heart Sandwiches

250 g (9 oz) strawberries
100 g (3½ oz) cream cheese

EGG MAYONNAISE
3–4 eggs
2 tablespoons mayonnaise
salt and pepper, to taste
shallots (scallions), sliced

GUACAMOLE
2 avocados
1 tablespoon lemon juice
salt and pepper, to taste
1 tomato, finely diced

CHOCOLATE AND BANANA
chocolate spread, like Nutella
2-3 bananas, peeled and sliced

Blend the strawberries and cream cheese in a food processor as a tasty filling in sandwiches. Use a heart cookie cutter to cut them into heart shapes.

Roll your favourite fillings, like ham or cucumber and cream cheese into soft Lebanese flatbread. Place filling to cover the whole surface of the flatbread. Roll up tightly and cut into 1–2cm (⅓–¾in) pieces. Roll up and cut into 'snails'. You can also have your bakery cut your bread loaf lengthways and fill the same way.

OTHER FILLINGS

EGG MAYONNAISE
Bring a pan of water to the boil. Gently submerge the room-temperature eggs into the boiling water. Boil for 8 minutes. Drain and allow to cool for 10 minutes. Peel the eggs and add the mayonnaise, salt pepper and some sliced shallots.

GUACAMOLE
Mash the avocadoes in a bowl and mix in the rest of the ingredients.

CHOCOLATE AND BANANA
Spread sandwiches with chocolate spread and place fresh banana slices on top of the spread.

White Crackles

Makes 24

300 g (9 oz) solid vegetable
    shortening/Crisco or Copha
200 g (7 oz) white chocolate
2 cups (80 g) Rice Krispies/Bubbles
1 cup desiccated (dry, unsweetened,
    shredded) coconut
225 g (8oz) icing (confectioners')
    sugar

Melt the shortening in a large pan over a medium heat.

Stir in the chocolate until it melts. Remove from heat and leave to cool for 10 minutes.

Add the remaining ingredients and mix well.

Spoon into cupcake cases and refrigerate until set—about 1–2 hours.

Chocolate Crackles

Makes 15

200 g (7 oz) vegetable shortening/
    Crisco or Copha
3 tablespoons Dutch dark cocoa
    powder
3 cups Rice Krispies/Bubbles
1 cup icing (confectioners') sugar
3/4 cup desiccated coconut

Melt the shortening in a large pan over a medium heat.

Stir in the cocoa. Remove from heat and leave to cool for 10 minutes.

Add the remaining ingredients and mix well.

Spoon into cupcake cases and refrigerate until set—about 1–2 hours.

Pink Crackles

Makes 24

300 g (10½ oz) solid vegetable
  shortening/ Crisco or Copha
200 g (7 oz) white chocolate
1 teaspoon pink food colouring
2 cups (80 g) Rice Krispies/Bubbles
1 cup desiccated (dry, unsweetened,
  shredded) coconut
225 g (8 oz/1 cup) icing
  (confectioners') sugar
3 tablespoons coloured sprinkles

Melt the shortening in a large pan over a medium heat.

Stir in the chocolate and allow to melt. Stir in the pink colouring until combined. Remove from heat and leave to cool for 10 minutes.

Add the remaining ingredients, except the sprinkles, and mix well.

Spoon into cupcake cases, top with sprinkles and refrigerate until set—about 1-2 hours.

Princess Maggie Cake

2 x 340 g (12 oz) packets butter
   cake mix
2 quantity Buttercream Frosting (see
   Basic Recipes)
yellow icing paste
240 g (8½ oz) fondant
blue icing paste
orange icing paste
purple icing paste
icing (confectioners') sugar, for
   dusting
DECORATIONS
8 fruit sticks
fruit chews
1 doll, legs removed

Preheat oven to 180°C/350°F/Gas mark 4 and butter and line the cake tin.

Prepare packets of cake mix, following directions on packet, and pour into a pudding basin tin 19.5cm (7¾in) in diametre, 5.5cm (2in) deep. Bake for 30 minutes, cover with foil and bake for another 30 minutes. Test with a skewer to make sure the cake is cooked. Leave to cool for 10 minutes, then turn onto a wire rack.

While cake cools, colour the butter frosting pale yellow. Divide the fondant into three portions and colour one portion blue, one orange and one purple.

Use a serrated knife to level the bottom of the cake. Using a palette knife, frost the cake yellow and decorate.

On a surface dusted with icing sugar, roll out the purple and orange fondant to 5mm (⅛in) thick. Using different-sized star cutters, cut out stars to decorate the cake. Roll out the blue fondant and make the doll's top and bow and place on top of cake.

Superhero Parties

Superhero Parties

This high-energy theme is a good one for very active children. Don't be fooled into thinking that this party is only for boys; girls have just as much fun learning to be a superhero and putting their superpowers to the test.

Ideal age group: 3+ years

Decorations

The superhero theme is all about being big and brave! Using bright colours to decorate will really help bring out the theme at the party. For place settings, cut stars out of cardboard—star stencils are readily available from arts and crafts stores, or online. Cover the stars in kitchen foil to create silver stars. Use the stars as placemats on your party table or hang them from the ceiling by punching a hole in one point and threading through a piece of string.

Hint...

If you want to create a superhero tablecloth, do it at the beginning of the party so it has time to dry. You'll need a long piece of inexpensive red material to cover the table and a selection of fabric paints. Once the children have arrived at the party, have them decorate the tablecloth so that it looks like a superhero's cape. Once they finish, allow the tablecloth to dry while the children play games. Once it's time for lunch the tablecloth should be dry and the kids will love seeing their superhero cape on the table.

As always, balloons are an awesome way to bring a theme and colour scheme together. Choose two or three different colours and place the balloons in bunches around the room.

Finally for the brave mums and dads, netting on the walls and police tape can help create a 'crime scene' where the superheroes will have to catch the villain.

Check
- Star placemats.
- Hanging superhero stars.
- Superhero 'cape' tablecloth
- Balloons.
- Wall netting.
- Police tape to create a crime scene.

Activities

The Superhero theme demands high–energy activities to get the kids running around.

1 Superhero Assault Course

Test the kids' superhero skills as they tackle the superhero assault course. They'll face several challenges and need all their superpowers to complete this game. You can add your own ideas and make the course as long and as complicated as you have space for.

You will need:

large blanket or sheet
small traffic cones or other tall objects
wooden beam/plank (optional)
hula hoops
large container
bean bags or similar
skipping rope

Establish a start point for the assault course. Open out the blanket and arrange it on the ground. The first obstacle is for the children to crawl under the blanket and come out the other side. If you want to make it harder, tell the children they can only crawl on their stomachs.

Next each child must do 5 star jumps.

Set the cones up in a slalom. The kids must run through them as quickly as possible.

Walk the plank without falling off.

Set out hula hoops in a line. The children must jump from one hoop to the next without stepping outside the hoop.

Using a large container as a target, see how many bean bags (or similar) the children can successfully throw into it.

Finally sprint to the finish line (the skipping rope held between two chairs).

Add in:

an egg and spoon race.
carrying a soft object, such as a cushion, on the head.

skip over a rope 10 times.

bounce a ball 10 times.

to make the assault course even more challenging, you can use a stopwatch to test the little superheroes' speed. however, always remember that games should be about having fun!

2 Cape Creators

Every superhero needs a cape. Even the little ones. Why not use this fun and creative idea to let the children create their own superhero capes to take home.

You will need:

capes, cut from large pieces of fabric (all they need to do is tie at the front and hang down at the back when worn)

fabric scissors

fabric paints

paint brushes

water

When the children arrive at the party hand each child a cape. The children can then use the fabric paints to design their very own superhero capes. Hang them up to dry so they will be ready to be taken home at the end of the party.

3 Everyone can be a Superhero

Being a superhero means being very cool, having super powers and being very fast. You also need to be very good at saving people. In this game each child can play the hero.

You will need:

lots of energy

In essence this is a game of tag with a twist. One player is selected to be the villain and must run around tagging (tapping on the shoulder) the other children. If a child is tagged, he or she must stand in a star shape until a superhero player saves him or her by crawling through the legs. Once a superhero has crawled through a tagged persons legs, the tagged person is free and able to be a superhero for someone else.

The aim of the game is for the baddie to tag everyone and for the superheroes to stop him. If there are a lot of children playing you can increase the number of villains. You can also change the way the superheroes save people. Instead of crawling through the legs, they might have to run under their arms instead.

4 Monster charge

This is best played outdoors with a large number of children.

Select a volunteer to be a monster. The children stand at one end of the space and when the monster shouts 'superheroes run' each player has to run past the monster to the other end of the space. If the monster catches anyone, they too become a monster. The game begins again. The aim is to be the last superhero, capable of ducking and diving past all the monsters. The last superhero in the game becomes the first monster of the next game.

5 Chopstick Dash

A team game of speed and skill, the aim is to move small objects with the aid of chopsticks, or other awkward tools, from a start point to a finish point some distance away.

You will need:

4 designated stations; 2 for the start and 2 for the end
pairs of small objects such as table tennis ball, sweets, cardboard tubes, pieces of dried pasta, etc
2 pairs of chopsticks, forks, spoons etc, table tennis bats
space

Place two stations at one end of the space and two at the other. Divide the pairs of objects between the start point stations. Divide the children into two teams and give the first player in each team a pair of chopsticks. When the game starts the first child in each team must pick up one object at a time with the chopsticks and carry it to the end station. At the end station he or she runs back to the start station and picks up the next object in the same way. The game continues until the first player has moved all the objects to the end station. He or she hands over the chopsticks to the second player who runs to the end station and must bring each object back to the start station, one at a time until all the objects have been retrieved. The player passes the chopsticks on to the third player. The winning team is the one that moves the objects fastest. The more awkward the objects to be moved the more skill the players require.

6 What Time Is It, Mr Wolf?

A hilarious game that will have children tiptoeing forward towards Mr Wolf and scurrying away again quickly to avoid being dinner!

One player is nominated to be Mr Wolf. He or she stands with his back towards the rest of the children, who stand in a line any distance away from him. Together they shout 'What time is it, Mr Wolf?' Mr Wolf turns to face the players and shouts back his choice of time, for example, 'It's 9 o'clock'. The children take the corresponding number of steps towards Mr Wolf. Mr Wolf turns his back again and the children again shout the question. As they get within touching distance of Mr Wolf and ask the time, Mr Wolf replies 'It's dinner time' and with that the children scarper back to the start line. If Mr Wolf catches a child, though, they become the next Mr Wolf.

Superhero Cake

Lightning Bolt Buttercake

Serves 12-20

450 g (1 lb) self-raising (self-rising)
    flour
20 ml (4 teaspoons) baking powder
250 g (9 oz) butter, softened
200 g (7 oz) margarine
10 ml (2 teaspoons) vanilla extract
450 g (1 lb) caster (superfine) sugar
6 large eggs, at room temperature
apricot or strawberry jam
2 portions of yellow Buttercream
    Frosting (see Basic Recipes)
1 portion of Royal Icing, for piping or
    red fondant (see Basic Recipes)
edible purple food colouring (optional)
black fondant

Preheat the oven to 180°C/350°F/Gas mark 4
    Lightly grease and line 2 rectangular cake
tins (pans) (35 x 20cm / 14 x 8in).
    Sift the flour and baking powder into a large
mixing bowl.
    Cream the butter, margarine, vanilla and
sugar in an electric mixer until pale and creamy.
Add the eggs one at a time. Add all the flour and
baking powder mixture and fold through using a
wooden spoon. Divide the mixture into prepared
cake tins and bake for 25 minutes or until the
edges pull away from the sides of the tin. Leave
to set for 10 minutes, then turn out on to a wire
rack to cool. Refrigerating the cake for several
hours will make cutting it easier.
    From one cake, trim all the edges for a neat
rectangle with straight edges. Cut the cake into
two triangles by making a cut from one corner to
the opposite corner. You will have two triangles
with one side almost twice the length of the other
side. Cut out a rhombus from the other cake—
that's two straight edges parallel to each other,
down the longest length of the rectangular cake
and across the cake another two parallel lines at a
30–45 degree angle from the other parallel lines.
See template. Place each triangle at either end of
the rhombus to make a lightning bolt. You will
need to cut sections out of the triangles at the
right angle corners to fit around the rhombus.

Once you have your shape, apply a rough coating of buttercream icing all over the cake, then refrigerate for a few hours. This will help stop the crumbs and allow a nice icing finish. Decorate your lightning bolt either using the royal icing flooding method, or using your template cut from rolled out fondant. Cut out letters from rolled out black fondant to form words like pow! and boom! Or you can paint these on using edible paint. Cut out your child's initials or name from paper glued to wire and placed in the cake. You can also decorate using your favourite superhero colours.

Power Lemonade Kryptonite Shots

Serves 6-8

POWER LEMONADE

3-4 different coloured cordials
1.25 litres (2½ pints) lemonade

Serves 12

KRYPTONITE SHOTS

1 packet green jelly

POWER LEMONADE
Remember to make these the day before so your ice cubes will freeze.

Make different coloured ice cubes, by adding a little coloured cordial to some water. Make 3–4 different colours, the more the better! When you're ready to serve, place 2 of each colour ice cube into a glass of lemonade. As the ice cubes melt the lemonade will turn different colours.

KRYPTONITE SHOTS
Make green jelly following the instructions on the packet, but adding an extra third (150ml/5fl oz) of the amount of water. Pour into small plastic cups or plastic shot glasses, about and set in the fridge for a few hours. Serve with a straw.

Pow! Sandwiches

Serves 6-10

chocolate spread or jam
1 loaf bread
1 packet pop rocks

Simple yet effective, the kids will get a real kick out of these.

Spread some chocolate spread or jam onto bread, sprinkle with pop rocks, place another piece of bread on top to make a sandwich. You could cut the sandwiches into shapes like emblems or lightning bolts. When the kids eat them they'll get a real surprise as each mouthful goes Pow!

Brownies

Makes 12

250 g (9 oz) butter

200 g (7 oz) milk or dark
   compound chocolate

30 ml (2 tablespoons) Dutch cocoa
   powder

300 g (10½ oz) caster (superfine)
   sugar

4 eggs

150 g (5 oz) plain (all-purpose)
   flour, sifted

50 g (1¾ oz) ground almonds
   (almond meal)*

Preheat the oven to 180°C/350°F/Gas mark 4.
Line a 20cm (7¾in) x 12cm (4¾in) x 3cm (1in)
deep tray with non-stick paper.

Melt the butter and the chocolate in a large
heatproof bowl set over a pan of gently simmering
water.

Stir in the cocoa, remove bowl from heat and
allow to cool.

Place the caster sugar, eggs, flour and ground
almonds into a stand mixer. Add the chocolate
mixture and stir to combine.

Pour into the tray and bake for 35 minutes.

Allow to cool completely. Refrigerate for a few
hours or overnight. Turn out onto a large cutting
board and cut into 12 squares.

*You may replace the ground almonds with 50g
(1¾ oz) plain flour if you wish to have a nut-free
brownie.

Pizza Rolls

Makes 24

DOUGH

250 ml (9 fl oz) lukewarm
    water
½ teaspoon sugar
16 g (½ oz) active dry yeast
740 g (1 lb 10 oz) strong
    white bread flour
1 teaspoon salt
10 ml (2 teaspoons) olive oil
1 egg
butter for greasing

FILLING

1 cup pizza sauce (see Whale
    Tail Pizzas)
1 cup grated mozzarella or
    pizza cheese
¼ cup pesto

Preheat the oven to 180°C/350°F/Gas mark 4. Line 2 baking trays with non-stick paper.

Make the dough by placing the water and sugar in a large bowl, and then sprinkle the yeast over the surface. Cover with a tea towel and leave for 5–10 minutes until foamy. Sift the flour and salt into the yeast mixture and mix with your hand until the mixture comes together and forms a dough. Knead for a few minutes in the bowl. Grease another large bowl with the olive oil. Place the dough into the bowl and cover with a clean kitchen towel. Leave in a warm place for 1 hour to 'prove'. Once doubled in size, turn out onto a clean, floured work surface and punch down the dough until it shrinks back to its original size. Divide the dough into two and place on an oiled baking dish. Cover and leave in a warm place for another 30 minutes. Punch down the dough again on a floured surface and knead for a minute. Grease a baking tray with more olive oil. Divide the dough into 4 balls, place on the tray 5cm (2in) apart and leave covered for a further 15–20 minutes.

On a clean, floured surface, use a rolling pin to gently roll each ball into a long, roughly oval shape (the shape doesn't have to be perfect) until the dough is 5mm ($^1/_8$in) thick. The width should be about 6cm (2in) and the length doesn't matter. Spread ¼ cup of sauce over the surface of each pizza, then a little pesto and finally ¼ cup of the cheese. Roll the dough up lengthways. Repeat for all pizzas. Cut each into 1cm ($^1/_3$in) slices, and lay flat onto the baking trays. Place in the oven and bake for 15-20 minutes or until golden. Allow to cool slightly before serving.

Mini Meat Pies

Makes 18

1 tablespoon olive oil

¼ cup onion, chopped

1 garlic clove, crushed

1 small carrot, peeled and grated

200 g (7 oz) ground (minced) beef

1 tablespoon tomato paste

2 teaspoons plain (all-purpose) flour

1 teaspoon Worcestershire sauce

½ cup beef stock

4 sheets (about 650 g/22 ¾ oz)
   puff pastry, almost thawed.

1 egg, beaten

Preheat oven to 180°C/350°F/Gas mark 4.

Heat oil in a medium fry pan. Over a medium heat, fry the onions, garlic and carrot for 1–2 minutes, stirring until soft. Add the mince and cook, stirring occasionally, until the meat is browned. Add the tomato paste, flour and Worcestershire sauce, stir and cook for a minute. Add the stock and cook, stirring for 5–8 minutes until sauce thickens. Allow to cool.

Grease an 18-hole mini muffin pan. Cut 18 cm (7 in) x 6 cm (2⅓ in) circles from half the pastry sheets. Line the muffin pan with the pastry circles. Fill each with the beef mixture, being careful not to fill past the rim. Cut 2½ cm (1 in) rounds from remaining pastry and place on top of the pies. Press the edges together. Brush the tops with a little egg and bake for 20 minutes or until golden. Allow to cool slightly before serving.

Mini Sausage Rolls

Makes 24

½ small onion, peeled

1 small carrot, peeled

1 tablespoon fresh parsley

1 garlic clove, peeled

300 g (10½ oz) ground (minced) beef

½ cup breadcrumbs

2 eggs

1 generous tablespoon tomato paste

1 tablespoon barbeque sauce

salt and pepper to taste

3 sheets (roughly 500 g/17½ oz) puff pastry, almost thawed

1 tablespoon poppyseeds (optional)

Preheat oven to 180°C/350°F/Gas mark 4. Line 2 baking trays with non-stick paper.

Place the onion, carrot, parsley and garlic into a food processor and chop finely.

Place the beef into a bowl. Add the onion mix, breadcrumbs, one egg, tomato paste, barbeque sauce, salt and pepper and mix well. Lay the puff sheets out and cut each into half.

Place the mince mixture along the centre of each half and roll up. Cut each into 4. Place onto baking trays leaving a little space between each. Whisk remaining egg lightly and brush over the top of each roll. Sprinkle with a pinch of poppyseeds if desired.

Bake for 25–30 minutes or until golden and puffed up. Allow to cool slightly before serving.

Krepe-tonite

Spinach and Chicken Crepe

Makes 10 large crepes
Serves 12-20

225 g (8 oz) plain (all-purpose) flour
½ teaspoon salt
4 large eggs
240 ml (8 fl oz) milk
240 ml (8 fl oz) water
55 g (2 oz) butter, melted, plus
   extra for brushing
cooking spray
1 bunch fresh spinach leaves, finely
   chopped
200 g (7 oz) fetta cheese, crumbled
100 g (3½ oz) roasted pumpkin,
   chopped
100 g (3½ oz) cooked chicken
   breast, shredded
1 tablespoon mayonnaise
1 teaspoon pesto (optional)

Sift the flour and salt into a bowl. Add the eggs and whisk to form a paste. Whisk in the milk, then the water, followed by the melted butter and mix until smooth.

Heat a large frying pan over a medium heat and lightly grease with cooking spray. Using a ladle, slowly drizzle the batter into the frying pan, tilting the pan back and forth to spread the batter thinly over the entire surface of the pan. Once bubbles start to appear over the entire surface, they are ready to flip (about 2 minutes). Fry for another 2 minute. Set aside. Continue until all the batter is used up. You can make these the day before, cover well with cling film and refrigerate.

Place the spinach, fetta, pumpkin, chicken, mayo and pesto in a bowl and mix. Place a handful onto each crepe along the centre in a line, and roll the crepes tightly. To serve, cut the crepes into circles.

Mini Chicken and Leek Pies

Serves 24

1 tablespoon olive oil

¼ cup leek, shredded

1 garlic clove, minced

1 teaspoon butter

1 teaspoon plain (all-purpose) flour

½ cup chicken stock

200 g (7 oz) chicken thigh, diced

1 tablespoon single cream

1 egg, beaten

4 sheets (650 g/22 ¾ oz) puff
   pastry, almost thawed.

Preheat oven to 180°C/350°F/Gas mark 4.

Heat oil in a medium frying pan. Over a medium heat, fry the leeks and garlic for 1–2 minutes, stirring until soft. Add the butter, then the flour and stir for 30 seconds. Add the chicken stock then bring to the boil, stirring. Add the chicken and the cream. Cook for 15 minutes until the chicken is cooked through and the sauce has thickened. Allow to cool.

Grease an 18-hole mini muffin pan. Cut 18cm (7in) x 6cm (2¹/₃in) circles from half the pastry sheets. Line the muffin pan with the pastry circles. Fill the pastry circles with the beef mixture ensuring not to fill past the rim. Cut 2½cm (1in) rounds from remaining pastry and place on top of pies. Press the edges together. Brush the tops with a little egg and bake for 20 minutes or until golden. Allow to cool slightly before serving.

X-ray Vision

Carrot and White Bean Dip

Serves 8-12

200 g (7 oz) carrots, peeled and cut
   into 1 cm (½ in) chunks
2 whole garlic cloves
1 tablespoon olive oil
400 g (14 oz) can cannellini or white
   beans
150 ml (5 fl oz) sour cream
juice of 1 lemon
salt and pepper, to taste

Preheat the oven to 180°C/350°F/Gas mark 4.
   Toss the carrots and whole garlic cloves in olive oil, decant into a roasting pan (tin) and roast in the oven for 20 minutes or until just soft. Blend in a food processor with the remaining ingredients until smooth. Serve with lavosh, bread, corn chips or vegetable sticks.

Fairy Parties

Fairy Parties

A typical choice of party for young girls but choosing the right colour scheme and selection of games will ensure that all of the children have a magical time.

Ideal age group: 3+ years

Decorations

The colour scheme you choose for this party is very important. If your guests are mostly girls, then you can go pink, pink, pink! However, if you are wanting to appeal to girls and the boys, use a more muted colour scheme such as the green and gold scheme of Tinker Bell's fairy dress.

Hang decorative butterflies from the ceiling.

Place vases of flowers on the table with decorative butterflies in the arrangement.

Use tulle as a tablecloth, to drape over the backs of chairs, the ceilings and walls to create a fairy forest effect.

Use small twinkling Christmas lights throughout the space to give the party that extra magical feel and for the brave parent, you could hire larger-than-life fake plants to add to the forest feel.

Check
- Hanging butterflies.
- Flower arrangements.
- Tulle tablecloths and draping.
- Butterfly placemats and wall hangings.
- Fake plants.
- Twinkling Christmas lights.

Activities

1 Painted Butterflies

You will need:

a butterfly shape drawn on paper for each child
a selection of colouring pencils, paints and paintbrushes

Draw the outlines of some butterflies on large sheets of paper and cut them out. Give one to each child as they arrive at the party and ask the children help you create decorations for the room. Invite the children to colour the butterflies using colouring pens, glitter, paints and any other materials you wish. When the butterflies are completed, use them as placemats or wall hangings for the party.

2 The Fairy Forest Hunt

As the children explore the fairy forest, why not take them on a fantastic adventure in search of magical hidden butterflies.

You will need:

toy butterflies

Before the children arrive and while the birthday child is not around, hide the toy butterflies throughout the party space. You can get very creative with your hiding places, such as in flower arrangements, under chairs, in plant pots, shoes, under furniture. Make sure you have enough butterflies for all of the children.

Ask the children to line up behind the birthday child then explain to them that throughout the Fairy Forest are small magical butterflies. Encourage them to find the butterflies as this will help them 'fly' just like fairies. Each child should find one butterfly that they can then take home with them. This is not only a fun and adventurous game. It is also a good way of handing out the party prizes.

3 Fairy Wands

Everyone knows that to be a real fairy you need a magic fairy wand. In this activity the children will have the chance to create their own.

You will need:

star shapes drawn on cardboard and cut out
wooden kebab (sharp ends removed) or paddle sticks
colouring pens / paints and paintbrushes
ribbon
glitter
scissors (child-safe)
sticky tape or glue

Give each child a star to decorate using colouring pens, paints, glitter or pencils. Encourage the children to make their wands as magical as possible. Once the children have completed their stars, encourage them to decorate the sticks. Use different colours of ribbon to wrap it around the sticks. Make sure that there is a small length of stick still showing. Glue each stick to the back of each star and leave to dry.

Remember...

Never leave children unattended with sharp objects.

4 The Fairy Forest Dance

This is a fun dance game that will get the children bobbing up and down while having a truly magical time.

You will need:

a music player and music

Play the music and have the children dance around the room like fairies. When the music stops the children must bop (crouch) to the ground. Play the games several times until the children understand how to play. Explain that the last 'fairy' to bop when the music stops will be out and will have to help you on the judging panel. Repeat the starting and stopping of the music until one child remains. The last child left is the winner.

5 Butterfly Nets

A game to play in a large space or outdoors, but not on a windy day!

You will need:

one butterfly net for each child
one balloon or ball-pit ball for each child

Played in pairs, each child collects a balloon in their net and has to keep it safe. The aim of the game is to nudge the other player's balloon out of their net and collect it in yours without losing yours. The winner is the one who retains the two balloons.

6 Pass the Parcel

This age-old favourite is perfect for any party. You can add theme-related punishment if the party is for older children, as well as sweet treats between the layers of wrapping paper, if you like.

You will need:

a small gift, wrapped with layers of gift wrap and between each layer you could add a sweet treat or a penalty/punishment
a source of music and someone to turn the music on and off

The players sit in a ring on the floor. As the music starts the parcel is passed in one direction from player to player. As the music stops the player holding the parcel must remove a layer of paper. It's a bittersweet game played in fear of having to perform a forfeit and in the hope of gaining a sweet treat. The game continues until the final layer of the parcel has been removed to reveal a gift for the person holding the parcel.

Suggested Penalty

Sing a nursery rhyme
Sing the chorus of a pop song by x
Say the alphabet backwards
Mew like a cat, bark like a dog, moo like a cow, etc
Swap socks with the person on your right
Give everyone a hug

All sing Merry Christmas to the tallest person in the circle

Do 10 star jumps

Hop till the music next stops

Pull a funny face

Variation: Create a fairy story in which different directions are repeated. The parcel (wrapped in a single layer of gift wrap) must pass in the direction given in the story. The longer the story, and the more directions given, the longer the game. Whoever is left holding the parcel at the story's end is the winner. For example, Tinkerbell decides to create mayhem and make herself dizzy. She takes three steps left, five steps right, two turns left before she remembers that she left her fairy purse in the Fairy Forest and has to retrace her steps to turn right, five steps left and three steps right before she gets back to her start point. She begins again holdig her purse in her right hand, but she's worried that she'll catch it on a flower so she moves it to her left hand before opening the bag with her right hand, stopping, turning right three times, then side stepping to the right…

Fairy Cake

Rainbow Butterfly Cake

Serves 20-30

500 g (18 oz) unsalted butter

500 g (18 oz) caster (superfine) sugar

15 ml (1 tablespoon) vanilla extract

10 eggs, beaten

175 g (6 oz) plain (all-purpose) flour, sifted

500 g (18 oz) self-raising (self-rising) flour, sifted

200 ml (7 fl oz) buttermilk

40 ml (1 ½ fl oz) milk

FROSTING

red, blue, green and yellow edible food colour

2 quantities Buttercream (see Basic Recipes)

2 quantities Royal Icing (see Basic Recipes)

decorator's or florist wire (optional)

fondant icing in various colours

edible glitter

Make the butterflies one day ahead. For the butterflies, tint balls of fondant icing in different colours. Roll out each to a thin sheet on a clean surface, lightly dusted with icing sugar. Stamp out different sizes of butterflies using cookie cutters. Make a concertina fold in some thick card and slip some of the butterflies into the dip, so that they set with their wings held aloft as if they are flying. Place in an airtight container and allow to dry overnight . You can also attach wire onto some of the butterflies while soft.

Preheat the oven to 160°C/325°F/Gas mark 3. Lightly grease and line six 24cm (9½in) round cake tins (pans).

Beat the butter in an electric mixer until pale and creamy, about 5–7 minutes. Slowly add the caster sugar, then the vanilla extract until the sugar is combined. Add the eggs one at a time, allowing each to be combined before adding the next. Scrape down the bowl occasionally. Add the flours, milk and buttermilk and mix by hand.

Divide the batter into 6 even portions in six bowls. Add a colour of the rainbow to each – red, orange (combine red and yellow), yellow, green, blue, and violet (combine blue and red). Bake each for 20–30 minutes, or until skewer comes out clean when inserted into the centre of the cake, or the cake sides come away from the edge of the tin.

Set aside the remaining colours covered in a cool place. When the first two are ready allow to cool for 5 minutes, then turn out onto a wire rack to go completely cold. Reline the two tins and continue cooking each colour layer. Trim the cakes so they are level and flat, then stack all the layers together, spreading a layer of buttercream between each.

Coat the stacked cake with buttercream and leave to set for a few hours. Cover with royal icing.

Just before serving, cover with some more royal icing and push each butterfly gently into the icing. Sprinkle the cake with edible glitter.

Fairy Bread

Serves 10-20

100 g (3½ oz/½ cup) sugar
120 ml (4 fl oz/½ cup) water
jam or chocolate spread
2 day-old loaves sliced white bread
edible glitter
hundreds and thousands or sprinkles

In a saucepan, combine the water and sugar and heat gently until the sugar dissolves. Turn up the heat and boil for 3 minutes until the syrup thickens. Set aside to cool.

Meanwhile, spread half the bread with jam or chocolate. Top each with another slice to make sandwiches. Use a butterfly cookie cutter to stamp out butterflies from the sandwiches.

Brush the tops of the sandwiches with cooled sugar syrup. Sprinkle with edible glitter or hundreds and thousands.

Magic Fairy Wands

Pink Macarons

Makes 8-12 wands

Macarons can take a little time to make. If you are in a hurry, use the cookie recipe for Easter to make star-shaped wands.

150 g (5 oz) icing (confectioners') sugar
85 g (3 oz) ground almonds (almond meal)
70 g (2¼ oz) egg whites, at room temperature and aged*
30 g (1 oz) caster (superfine) sugar
edible pink colouring
1 quantity Buttercream Frosting (see Basic Recipes), coloured pink
Royal Icing (see Basic Recipes) or melted white chocolate, for attaching the popsticks
popsticks (available from craft supply stores)

Preheat the oven to 160°C/325°F/Gas mark 3.

Sift the icing sugar and the ground almonds together into a large bowl a minimum of 3 times (the more times you sift the better).

In an electric mixer, whisk the egg whites until soft peaks form, reduce the mixer speed to low and slowly add the caster sugar, then a few drops of edible pink colouring. Increase the speed to medium and whisk until stiff peaks form.

Sift the icing sugar and ground almonds into the egg whites, then use a metal spoon to gently fold the mixture together until a glossy batter forms. Do not overmix the batter, about 45–50 gentle folds are enough The mixture should slide off your metal spoon very slowly.

Line two baking trays with wax paper.

Spoon the mixture into a piping bag and snip the end off to allow a 1 cm hole, the batter should not fall out of the piping bag without being squeezed. If it is, then your macarons have been overmixed. Pipe 2–3 cm (1–1 ½ in) circles onto a baking tray approximately 2 cm (¾ in) apart. If a peak is left, flatten it slightly with a wet finger. Tap the baking tray to release any air bubbles in the mixture. Set aside for at least one hour. A crust should form on the surface, which when touched lightly won't stick to your finger. They're ready to bake when they are at this stage

Turn down the oven to 140°C/275°F/Gas mark 1. Bake the macarons for 20–25 minutes or until they release easily from the tray without sticking. Allow to go cold.

Use a little royal icing or melted white chocolate to attach a popstick to the flat side of half of the macarons on the flat side. Coat the flat side with pink buttercream. Top with another macaron and leave to set for a few hours.

COOKIE DOUGH WANDS

If you are making star-shaped wands using the Festive Cookies recipe, use a cookie cutter to stamp out star shapes and bake according to the instructions. Use a little melted white chocolate to stick popsticks to the underside of the stars, making 'wands'. Use the 'flooding' method to decorate.

Colour some royal icing (use a gel colour if you can so it doesn't thin the royal icing too much. If using liquid colour add a little extra icing sugar to retain the consistency of the royal icing). Spoon some royal icing into a piping bag fitted with fine line piping tube. Pipe a border around the outside of the cookie. Allow to dry for 1 hour. Adding a little water 1 teaspoon at a time to the remaining icing sugar until you have a mixture that is a little runny. Fill another piping bag with runny icing and flood the cookie with the icing, taking care that it doesn't breach the piped border. Use a skewer or paintbrush to push the icing into the corners. Sprinkle with silver balls or stars or edible glitter. Allow to dry.

*Precise measurements are required for this recipe so it is best to measure the egg whites by weight rather than using a particular amount of eggs. 'Aged' means to allow the egg whites to 'rest' for several hours and even days (the longer the better). Place in the refrigerator for 24–48 hours, then leave outside to bring to room temperature before using.

OTHER IDEAS
Cook farfalle pasta as 'butterflies'.
Make toadstools by placing a fresh raspberry over a mini marshmallow on a bed of green.
Cut red apples in quarters and remove the seeds. Dot with melted chocolate to look like ladybirds.

Chocolate Cake Pops

Makes 25

½ small chocolate cake sponge
½ portion of chocolate buttercream
   icing
25 popsticks
500 g (17½ oz) milk compound
   chocolate

Using your fingers, crumble the cake into crumbs. Stir in the icing and mix well.

Roll into small balls, and place onto a tray lined with wax paper. Insert a popstick into each ball and refrigerate for 2–3 hours until firm.

Melt the chocolate separately over a double boiler. Coat each ball with the chocolate and insert the stick into a styrofoam block or similar to harden. Once all are coated, coat each with a second coat. Set in the fridge until ready to serve.

Ice Cream Pops

Makes 12

450 ml (15 fl oz) vanilla or chocolate
    ice cream (frozen firm)
12 paddle popsticks
300g (10½ oz) milk chocolate,
    chopped
2 teaspoons vegetable oil
coloured sprinkles for decorating

Line two baking trays with wax non-stick paper and place in the freezer to chill for a few hours.

Using a melon baller, scoop 12 balls of ice cream and place on one of the baking trays. Insert a paddle popstick into each and return to the freezer for several hours or until frozen.

Melt the chocolate over a double boiler. Remove from heat and stir in the oil until mixed. Allow chocolate to cool to room temperature.

Remove pops from the freezer and dip each one into the chocolate mixture one at a time, allowing excess chocolate to drip off. Sprinkle each with coloured sprinkles while chocolate is wet. Place the pops onto the other tray and return to the freezer until ready to serve. Serve straight from the freezer.

Butterfly Bruschetta

Serves 10-15

2 long French sticks

30 ml (2 tablespoons) extra virgin
    olive oil, plus extra for drizzling

6 ripe tomatoes, diced

1 red onion, finely chopped

½ bunch basil, leaves shredded

1 garlic clove, finely chopped

100 g (3½ oz) goat's cheese/curd

1 bunch chives

salt and pepper

Preheat the oven to 200°C/400°F/Gas mark 6.

Slice the French sticks into rounds and put on a baking tray. Brush lightly with extra virgin olive oil and bake in the oven for 10 minutes or until toasted. Set aside for 1 hour until the bread becomes crunchy.

In a bowl, mix together the diced tomatoes, onion, basil leaves and garlic and add a drizzle of olive oil. Season with salt and pepper. Smear each toasted round with bruschetta mix and goat's cheese. Arrange on a serving plate to look like butterflies. Add chives for antennae. Serve straightaway.

Toadstool Tartlets

Makes 24 tarts
Serves 8-12

spray oil
3 sheets (about 500-800 g/17½ -
    28 oz) ready-rolled shortcrust
    pastry
1 egg, lightly beaten
200 g (7 oz) fetta cheese, cubed
    into 24 pieces, reserve the crumbs
    of cheese caused by cutting
1 bunch basil, leaves only
12 cherry or baby tomatoes, halved

CARAMELISED ONIONS
10 ml (2 teaspoons) olive oil
2 onions, finely sliced
20 ml (4 teaspoons) balsamic
    vinegar
30 ml (2 tablespoons) light brown
    sugar

Preheat the oven to 190°C/375°F/Gas mark 5

Lightly grease a small muffin or tart tin with cooking spray. With a cookie cutter that is larger than the tins, stamp out circles from pastry sheets and line the muffin or tart tins. The tartlets should be quite shallow so the pastry doesn't have to come all the way up the sides. Trim away the excess pastry and re-roll to line the tin again. Brush with a little egg and bake in the preheated oven for 15 minutes, or until golden. Allow to cool.

Meanwhile, make the caramelised onions. Heat the olive oil in a saucepan over medium heat. Add the onions and cook until soft and translucent, about 5–10 minutes. Turn up the heat and add the balsamic vinegar. Stir to coat the onions. Add the brown sugar and cook until the liquid thickens and onions caramelise.

When you are ready to serve, place a whole basil leaf in a pastry case. Top with a ¼ tablespoon of onions. Top with a cube of cheese and a tomato half. Sprinkle with some of the leftover fetta crumbs for toadstool spots.

128

Jungle Parties

Jungle Parties

Jungle parties are a fabulous way to engage both boys and girls of mixed ages. Because the theme is so vast and you can include all kinds of different animals, you are sure to be able to find something that will please everyone.

Ideal age group: 1–8 years

Decorations

Hang fake vines throughout the room to create a jungle oasis.

Make toadstools by cutting out circles from cardboard and painting them red. Once they've dried, add white spots using paint and allow to dry. Arrange them on the floor throughout the space or use them as placemats on the table.

Hang fake butterflies from the ceiling or use them as place settings for the table.

Place toy frogs, monkeys or jungle animals through the room.

Using kids' fishing nets (with rods) as scene setters is also a fantastic idea. Fill a bucket with sand to hold the rods in place. Put treats in the nets if you like.

Buy some fake grass for the floor or to create a tablecloth.

Check
- Hanging vines
- Cardboard toadstool floor and placemats
- Hang fake butterflies throughout the room
- Fishing net room setters
- Fake grass tablecloths
- Fake grass floors.

Activities

With such a big theme, you have so many wonderful ideas to choose from.

1 Gone Fishing

If the children are going to be real jungle explorers, they will need to learn how to catch their own dinner. What better way than to 'fish' for it. This game is not just a test of skill, it's also good fun.

You will need:

2 large buckets

fishing net (with rod)

several rubber ducks or similar

water

Fill a bucket with water. Then explain to the children that to be a jungle explorer they need to be good at catching things. One at a time and standing behind a line or designated spot, they must each take the fishing net and try to catch as many rubber ducks within 30 seconds as possible. They can only pick one duck up at a time and must put them into the empty bucket next to the one with water. The child that collects the most ducks is the winner.

Remember...

Never leave children unattended with large amounts of water.'

2 The Toadstool Hop

This wild jungle game will have the children enjoying themselves so much and having lots of fun. It's a variation of musical chairs and fun to play with any children of any age. It can be played inside and out.

You will need:

cardboard toadstools (see jungle decoration ideas), one for each child

a music player

music

Arrange the toadstools around the space, making sure that they are spaced far apart. Explain to the children that when the music plays they must dance like their favourite jungle animal, but when the music stops they must find a toadstool to stand on.

Once the children are familiar with how the game is played, take away one of the toadstools so there is one more child than toadstool. Play the music again and when the music stops the child that doesn't reach a toadstool quickly enough has to stand out and help judge.

After each elimination remove another toadstool is removed until one remains with two children left to dash for it. The child to stand on the toadstool first when the music stops is the winner.

Variation: Encourage the children to dance like their favourite jungle animals to begin with, and then give them a specific animal to impersonate. The child that makes the most convincing impersonation is the winner.

3 Jungle Monster Maker

This arts and crafts idea allows the children to sit quietly and use their imagination. There really are no rules when it comes to the jungle and the same applies here.

You will need:

small empty plastic bottles, pierced on each side, approximately half way up, using
   scissors.
scissors (child safe)
coloured pipe cleaners
fluffy balls
stick-on eyes
felt
glue

Show the children how to feed the coloured pipe cleaners through the holes in the bottle to create arms. (Monsters can have many arms.) The children can then start to decorate their monsters using the materials provided. Felt, fluffy pompoms and stick-on eyes are fun ideas that will really help the monsters have a wild jungle look.

4 Sleeping Lions

All the children lie on the floor. They mustn't move a muscle or they'll be out of the game. A lion hunter (parent) attempts to make the children move or laugh by telling jokes, but mustn't touch anyone. The winner is the lion who remains still for the longest.

5 Fill the Well

A team game that is best played outside with plenty of space.

You will need:
2 buckets for each team
1 small container such as a plastic cup
sand or water to fill one of the buckets

Divide the group of children into two teams. Place the sand or water-filled bucket at one end of the space and put the container in it. Put the empty bucket at the other end of the space. When the game starts, the first player takes a cup of water or sand and dashes to the bucket at the other end of the space. He empties his cup into the bucket, dashes back to the start point and hands the container to the next team player. The second player fills the cup and dashes to the other end of the space and empties the container into the bucket. The game continues until a team has emptied the bucket at the start point and filled the other at the end point. In the event of a tie, the team with the fuller bucket and who have dropped least, wins.

Jungle Cake

Banana Cake

Serves 10-15

125 g (4 oz) butter, softened

150 g (5 oz) caster (superfine)
   sugar

15 ml (1 tablespoon) vanilla extract

2 eggs, at room temperature

185 ml (6½ fl oz) creamy yoghurt
   of your choice, full fat or light

1½ cups over-ripe bananas, mashed
   (approximately 4-5 bananas,
   depending on size)

260 g (9 oz) self-raising (self-rising)
   flour, sifted

¼ teaspoon bicarbonate of soda
   (baking soda)

200 g (7 oz) passionfruit
   buttercream

2 portions caramel-colour Royal Icing

50 g (1¾ oz) black fondant

300 g (10½ oz) white fondant plus
   extra for decorating

150 g (5 oz) light brown fondant

500 g (17½ oz) dark brown
   fondant

green colour paste

red colour paste

Preheat the oven to 180°C/350°F/Gas mark 4.
Lightly grease and line a 24 cm (10 in) round
cake tin (pan).

Beat the butter with electric beaters until
pale. Add the sugar and vanilla and beat until
thick and creamy.

Add the eggs, one at a time, allowing each to
be incorporated before adding the next. Scrape
down the bowl.

Add the yoghurt and banana and gently fold
into the sugar and butter mixture.

Add the flour and bicarbonate of soda and fold
in with a metal spoon until just combined.

Bake in the preheated oven for 50–60 minutes
or until a skewer comes out clean when inserted
into the centre. Leave to set for 10 minutes, then
turn out onto a wire rack to cool.

Once cold, cut the cake in half and spread a
layer of Passionfruit Buttercream on the bottom
half and sandwich the two cakes together. Place
the cake onto a plate or cake board and use the
remaining icing to cover the outside of the cake.
When dry, cover with Royal Icing and allow to set.

To make the monkey, roll out two long
sausages from dark brown fondant, long enough
to go around the entire cake. Flatten slightly
using a palette knife. Cut 2 grooves at each end
of each roll to form 2 hands and 2 feet. Place one
around the base of the cake and one on top.

Make a head by forming an egg shape also from dark brown fondant. Flatten one side with the back of a spoon. You should have one thick edge sloping down to a thin edge. Place the head, resting on the back of the arms. Roll out a large oval in light brown fondant for the chin. Place on, overlapping the head. Form some ears in light brown by rolling and flattening a small ball of fondant. Use a finger to make indents. Place between the head and arms. Make some eyes with white fondant.

Use black fondant for eyes, nostrils, mouth and belly button.

You can make leaves and bugs, flowers, lady beetles and caterpillars by moulding coloured fondant into shapes and allowing to set hard. Be creative and have fun.

Sweet Pachyderm

Elephant Meringues

Makes 12-18

6 egg whites, at room temperature

15 ml (1 tablespoon) cornflour
 (cornstarch)

10 ml (2 teaspoons) white vinegar

350 g (12 oz) granulated (white)
 sugar

black edible food colour

pink edible food colour

wafer cones

50 g (1¾ oz) white chocolate,
 melted

small quantity black piping icing

small quantity white piping icing

Preheat the oven to 100°C/200°F/Gas mark 1.

Whisk the egg whites in a clean, dry bowl until soft peaks form. Add the cornflour and vinegar, then add the sugar slowly, a little at a time. Divide the mixture in half. To one half, add a few drops of black colouring until you have 'elephant' grey. To the other half, add pink food colouring.

Scoop the mixtures into two large piping bags fitted with a nozzle with a 1cm (½in) hole. Line a baking tray with non-stick baking paper, then holding the bag upright, pipe circles of meringue for the elephant faces, keeping the nozzle tip touching the meringue until a 3cm (1¼in) circle is piped. Lift the piping bag upwards while continuing to pipe the trunks. Pipe the circles 2cm (¾in) apart. Bake for 2½ hours.

Break up the wafer cones into ear-shaped pieces and stick to the elephants' heads. Allow to cool for 2 hours. Using white and black icing, pipe eyes onto the faces. You can also make fondant eyes in advance and 'glue' them on with melted white chocolate.

Jungle Jumble Cupcakes

Makes 12

150g (5oz) butter, at room
    temperature
1 cup caster (superfine) sugar
3 eggs
1 teaspoon vanilla extract
½ cup milk
1½ cups self-raising (self-rising) flour,
    sifted
300 g (10½ oz) fondant
green icing paste
Royal Icing (see Basic Recipes)
icing (confectioners') sugar

DECORATIONS

12 snakes
24 freckles, nonpareils or jazzles
12 mini frogs
12 tropical sweets
12 mint leaves
12 liquorice bullets

Preheat the oven to 160°C/325°F/Gas mark 3 and line a 12-cup muffin tray with cupcake papers.

Cream butter and sugar together until light and fluffy. Add eggs one at a time, beating well after each addition. Add the vanilla.

Add half the milk and half the flour, mix, then add the remaining milk and flour. Divide the mixture evenly between the cupcake papers.

Bake for 20 minutes until cooked. Cool for 5 minutes, then turn onto a cooling rack.

Colour the fondant green. Spread a small amount of royal icing on top of each cupcake—this will secure the fondant.

On a surface dusted with icing sugar, roll out fondant to 5mm (⅛ in) thick. Using a round cutter, cut 12 circles from the fondant. Place each circle on top of a cupcake. Attach the decorations to each cupcake.

Gina the Giraffe

4 x 340 g (12 oz) packets
    butter cake mix
2 quantity Buttercream
    Frosting (see Basic Recipes)
orange icing paste
brown icing paste
red icing paste

DECORATIONS
½ cup chocolate sprinkles
1 white baby marshmallow,
    cut in half
2 giant black Smarties
2 chocolate-covered sweets
2 brown Smarties

Preheat oven to 180°C/ 350°F/Gas mark 4 and butter and line the cake tins.

Prepare 2 packets of cake mix, following directions on packet, and pour into a 22cm (8½in) round cake tin. Prepare remaining 2 packets of cake mix and fill a 17.5 x 12.5cm (6¾ x 5in) rectangular tin. Bake for 30 minutes, cover with foil and bake for another 30 minutes. Test with a skewer to make sure the cakes are cooked. Leave to cool for 10 minutes, then turn onto a cooling rack.

While cakes cool, divide frosting in half, colour one half orange. Divide the remaining frosting in half, colour one half brown and the remaining half pale pink.

Use a serrated knife to level the cakes. Using the template following the recipe, cut a section out of the round cake and discard—this is where the nose will go. Cut ear and nose from rectangular cake. Stand the nose on its end and shape the edges to fit into the round cake. Cut ear in half horizontally to make two.

Using a palette knife, frost the head with orange. Frost the nose and ears with brown. Frost the middle of the ear with pale pink, using your finger to pat down. Attach to the head with skewers and frosting.

Using different-sized round cutters, mark out the dots on the giraffe, then fill each dot with the chocolate sprinkles. Attach the marshmallow halves to the giant Smarties with frosting, position on cake. Position the choc-covered candy and brown Smarties in place. If necessary, fill a piping bag with leftover frosting and seal the joins of the nose and ears.

Gina the giraffe A4 size template • part A

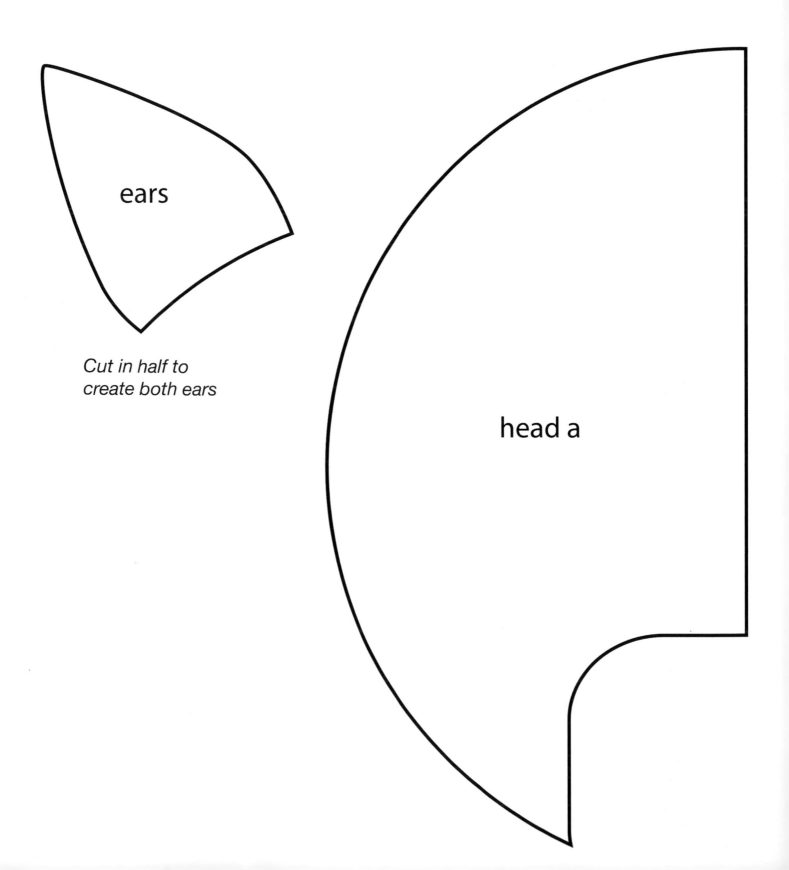

ears

Cut in half to
create both ears

head a

Gina the giraffe

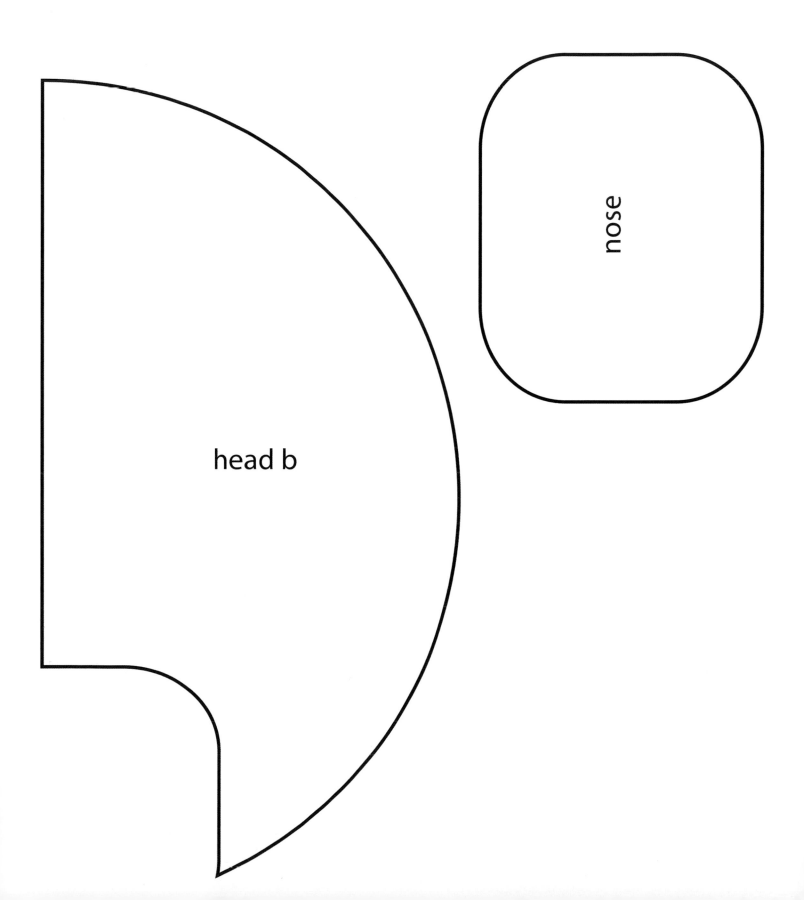

head b

nose

Zephyr the Zebra

4 x 340 g (12 oz) packets butter
   cake mix
2 quantity Buttercream Frosting
   (see Basic Recipes)
black icing paste
red icing paste

DECORATIONS

1 white baby marshmallow, cut in
   half
2 giant black Smarties
10 pieces soft liquorice

Preheat oven to 180°C/ 350°F/Gas mark 4 and butter and line the cake tins.

Prepare 2 packets of cake mix, following directions on packet, and pour into a 22cm (8½in) round cake tin. Prepare remaining 2 packets of cake mix and pour into a 17.5 x 12.5cm (6¾ x 5in) rectangular cake tin. Bake for 30 minutes, cover with foil and bake for another 30 minutes. Test with a skewer to make sure the cakes are cooked. Leave to cool for 10 minutes, then turn onto a cooling rack.

While cakes cool, divide frosting in half, leave half plain. Divide remaining frosting in half again and colour one half black and the other half pink.

Use a serrated knife to level the cakes. Using the template following this recipe, cut a section out of the round cake and discard—this is where the nose will go. Cut ear, mane and nose from rectangular cake. Stand the nose on its end and shape the edges to fit into the round cake. Cut ear in half horizontally to make two.

Using a palette knife, frost the head with plain frosting. Frost the nose, mane and ears with black, and frost the middle of the ear with pink. Attach to the head with skewers and frosting.

Attach the marshmallows to the giant Smarties with icing, then place on cake as the eyes. Cut 2 slices off 1 piece of liquorice and position on nose for nostrils. Roll the remaining liquorice out flat, cut out stripes and attach with frosting. If necessary, fill a piping bag with leftover frosting and seal the joins of the nose, mane and ears.

Zephyr the zebra • A4 size template • part A

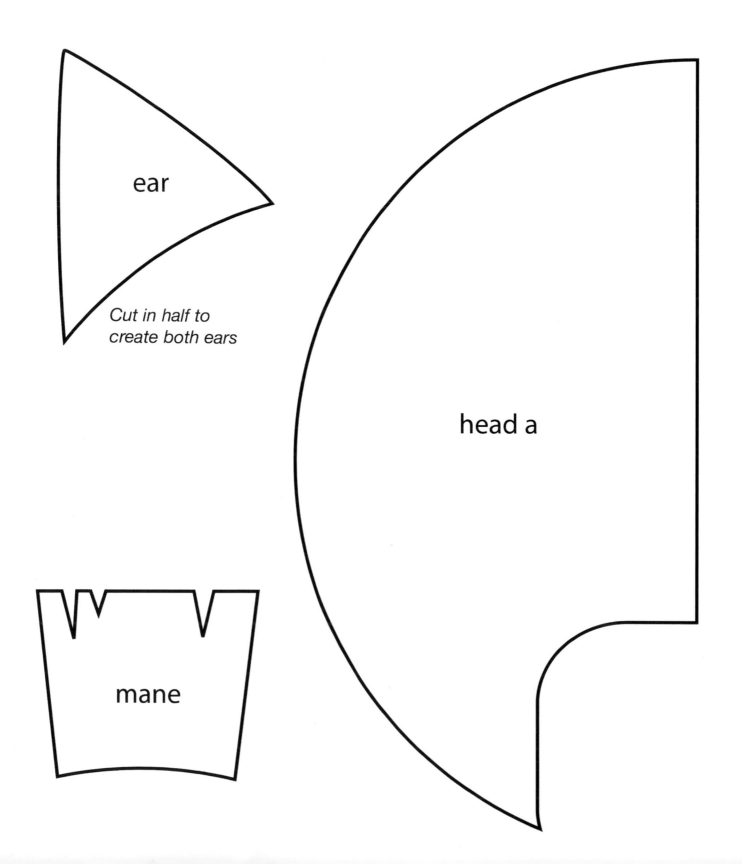

ear

Cut in half to create both ears

head a

mane

Zephyr the zebra

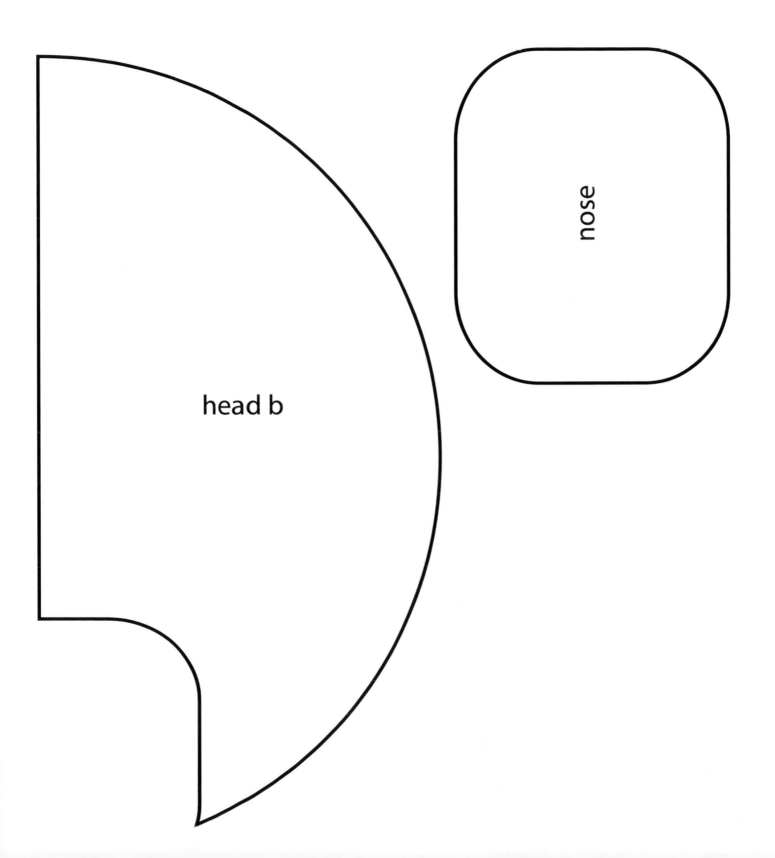

head b

nose

Snail Bread

Makes 6-12

7 g (1 packet) dry active yeast
10 ml (2 teaspoons) sugar
250 ml (9 fl oz) warm water
750 g (1 lb 10 oz) strong white
    bread flour, plus extra for dusting
10 ml (2 teaspoons) salt
15 ml (1 tablespoon) olive oil
1 egg, lightly beaten
ham and cheese, to fill

Put the yeast, sugar and water in a bowl and set aside for 10 minutes until frothy.

Sift the flour and salt into a mixing bowl. Add the yeast mixture and mix until a dough forms. Knead on a lightly floured surface for 5–10 minutes. The dough should still be a little sticky (add a little bit more water if you need to).

Grease a clean bowl with the olive oil. Add the dough, then cover with a tea towel and put in a warm place. Leave for 1 hour or until the dough doubles in size. On a lightly floured work surface knock back (punch down) the dough for a few seconds until it returns to its original size. Cut into 4 pieces, cover again and leave in a warm place for 20 minutes.

Cut each quarter into 3 or 4 pieces. Gently roll each into a sausage, flatten slightly and roll into a snail. Place each snail onto a tray lined with baking paper and leave, covered in a warm place, for another 15 minutes.

Preheat the oven to 200°C/400°F/Gas mark 6.

Brush with a little egg and bake for about 12-18 minutes. Serve as they are or fill with ham and cheese, and bake for another 3 or 4 minutes.

OTHER IDEAS
Thread grapes onto long skewers, draw eyes on one end with melted white chocolate for 'caterpillers' (make sure to cut the pointy ends off the skewers).
Float blueberries in lemonade as 'bug juice'.
Top crackers with cream cheese, half a cherry tomato and an olive as lady beetles.

Wedges

Serves 5-10

500 g (17½ oz) large, washed
    potatoes cut into 1.5 cm (½ in)
    thick wedges
1 teaspoon olive oil
1 tablespoon seasoning salt
sour cream, for serving
sweet chilli sauce, for serving

Preheat oven to 200°C/400°F/Gas mark 6.

Place the cut wedges into a large saucepan, cover with cold water and bring to the boil. Turn down to a simmer and cook the potatoes for 6–8 minutes. Drain and lay on a kitchen towel to dry for 10 minutes.

Grease a baking tray with the oil and spread potato pieces onto the tray ensuring they are flat and not piled on top of each other. Place into the oven for 20 minutes, turn all the pieces and bake a further 10 minutes or until golden. Toss lightly in the seasoning salt and serve with sour cream and sweet chilli sauce.

Cheese Puffs

Makes 24

3 tablespoons (40 g) butter, cubed
½ cup water
¼ teaspoon salt
½ cup plain (all-purpose) flour
2 eggs
¾ cup grated cheese
4 tablespoons chives, finely chopped

Preheat oven to 220°C/425°F/Gas mark 7.

Measure all ingredients out, as you will need to work quickly.

Line two baking trays with non-stick paper.

Place the butter, water and salt in a medium pot. Over medium heat, melt ingredients together. When combined, add the flour, and mix until a dough ball forms.

Allow to cool, then place in a large clean bowl. Using an electric mixer, beat in the eggs one at a time until combined. Mix in the cheese and chives.

Roll into 24 2-cm (¾in) wide balls, and place onto trays 1 cm (¹/3in) apart. Bake for 10 minutes, then turn down the oven to 190°C/375°F/Gas mark 5 and cook for a further 20–25 minutes until golden. Allow to cool slightly before serving.

Forest Fodder

Fennel and Bacon-stuffed Mushrooms with Haloumi

Serves 12

12 cup or field mushrooms

1 baby fennel bulb, sliced

50 g (1¾ oz) smoked bacon, diced

1 tablespoon olive oil

100 g (3½ oz) ricotta cheese

1 egg

20 g (¾ oz) Parmesan, grated

15 ml (1 tablespoon) pine nuts,
   toasted

6 basil leaves, shredded

50 g (1¾ oz) breadcrumbs

100 g (3½ oz) butter, cubed

1 garlic clove, sliced

12 slices (about 600 g/21 oz)
   haloumi

1 lemon

salt and pepper

Preheat the oven to 180°C/350°F/Gas mark 4.

Gently wipe the mushrooms with a damp kitchen towel. Remove and dice the stems.

Lightly fry the fennel, diced mushroom stems and smoked bacon in a little olive oil, until soft.

In a bowl, mix together the fennel and bacon mixture, ricotta cheese, egg, Parmesan, pine nuts, basil, breadcrumbs and salt and pepper. Stuff each mushroom with the ricotta mix and place on a baking tray. Put the butter in the tray around the mushrooms with the sliced garlic.

Bake for 10–15 minutes, then remove from the oven. Put a slice of haloumi on top of each mushroom, squeeze a little lemon over and grill for 3–4 minutes under a hot grill until golden. Serve straightaway.

Birds of Paradise

Rice Paper Rolls

Makes 12

3 shallots/green onion, sliced

100 g (3½ oz) rice vermicelli
    noodles

50 g (1¾ oz) roasted peanuts,
    crushed (optional) or Asian fried
    onions

30 ml (1 oz) coriander, chopped

30 ml (1 oz) mint, chopped

1 cucumber, sliced and trimmed into
    36 batons

2-3 carrots, peeled and sliced into
    36 batons

12 round rice papers

50-100 g (1¾ - 3 ½ oz) smoked
    trout, shredded

½ bunch coriander leaves

½ bunch mint leaves

SAUCE

120 ml (2 fl oz) sweet soy sauce
    (kecap manis)

120 ml (2 fl oz) sweet chilli sauce

120 ml (2 fl oz) light soy sauce

30 ml (1 oz) fish sauce (nam pla)

juice of 2 lemons

Put all the sauce ingredients in a food processor and blend until combined.

Place the sliced shallots in 240 ml (8 fl oz /2 cups) iced water and leave for 5–10 minutes to curl.

Put the rice vermicelli noodles in a bowl and cover with boiling water. Leave for 5 minutes to soften then drain well and leave to cool.

Combine the noodles, peanuts and chopped herbs along with 2–3 tablespoons of the prepared sauce and mix well.

Fill a large bowl with hot, but not boiling, water. Dip one rice paper circle in and leave for a few seconds until just the edges start to soften. Place rough side down on a clean work bench. Starting in the centre of the circle, place a small handful of noodles all the way to the top, so you have one strip, which is the radius of the circle. On top of the noodles, place 3–4 pieces of carrots, same of cucumber and shallots, 3–4 leaves of coriander and mint. Now grab the edge of the left side of the paper and wrap it over the filling, coming in tight at the bottom and loose at the top. Now grab the bottom of the circle and drape it over the filling tightly. Now grab the right edge of the circle, and wrap it over to form an open-ended roll. Repeat until you have desired amount of rolls. Serve immediately, or cover with a damp cloth for 2 hours (not in the fridge) before serving. Serve the sauce on the side as a dipping sauce.

Witches & Wizards Parties

Witches and Wizards Parties

This super-spooky theme is ideal for boys and girls and makes a perfect halloween party. You can vary the spookiness based on the ages of the children.

Ideal age group: 5+ years

Decorations

This is a truly fantastic theme to work with when it comes to decorating. Just let your creative juices flow. The internet is a fabulous source of Halloween party decorations—you can even buy cobwebs and larger-than-life spiders to use. Use fallen leaves and twigs to set the scene, fashion witches' brooms and set up cauldrons throughout the room and fill them with all kinds of spooky treats. Hanging 3-dimensional spiders and bats from the ceiling, or using flat cut-out ones for place settings adds a wonderful touch. Put electric candles in paper bags to give the lighting an eerie feel. You can even buy fake eye balls and scatter them over the table.

If you can buy inflatable skeletons or replica skull and bones it will add to the feel. You could hang them around the space, or even set them up at the table. Discount shops even sell inflatable 'coffins' at Halloween and you could use these to fill with water for apple bobbing.

For those who want to go one step further, then renting a dry ice machine will really give the party a scary feel. Call your party room the 'room of doom'.

Hint
Always make sure the room is well ventilated.

Activities

This theme can be scary for some younger children so keep the games and the decorations appropriate for the ages of the children.

1 Guts Galore

A gruesome game where the children can only use their sense of touch to feel their way to success. This game is great fun and the children will love getting stuck in.

You will need:

several buckets

water

flour

corn flakes

spaghetti (cooked)

fake eye balls

custard

baked beans or spaghetti hoops

jelly

bright food colour

sealed-wrapper sweets

blindfold

Play the game in an area that you can wash down later.

Before the party fill the each bucket with different ingredients to create your gruesome guts bowls. Add some colouring to the content in scary colours and mix in well. For example, add red food colour to the custard bucket to make it look like blood. In each bucket bury several sweets, which should be wrapped in sealed wrappers, so that they don't spoil.

Have a towel handy for after the game.

Explain to the children that the buckets are filled with gruesome guts and in order to claim their prizes they will have to place their hands into the buckets to fish them out. To add another fun element, you may wish to blindfold the children and give them a time limit to find the prizes (you could add booby prizes too).

2 Apple Bobbing Madness

This is a fun and classic game with a spine-tingling twist that the children will love playing. You can make this game as scary as you like, but just make sure that the children are always supervised.

large bucket
water
red food colouring
small apples, washed
fake eye balls

Fill the bucket with water. Add the red food colouring to give the water the look of blood. Add the apples and the fake eye balls.

   Explain to the children that with their hands behind their back, they must try and grab as many apples from the 'blood'-filled bucket as they can, using only their teeth. Tell them they have just 60 seconds each. The child who pulls the most apples from the bucket is the winner. Remind the children to avoid the eerie eye balls.

Remember..
Never leave children unattended with large amounts of water.

3 The Witch Stitch Limbo

This game is great to play with a large group of children as it allows each child to have several turns. It's also lots of fun for a whole host of ages.

You will need:
witches broomstick
music player
music

This game is run like a classic game of limbo. Have the children line up behind the birthday child and have two adults hold up the broom stick at each end. When the music starts the children must make their way under the broomstick (limbo) and join the back of the line. Every time the birthday child comes back around, the broom stick is lowered. The idea of the game is to see how low can they go!

4 Halloween Relay

A good game to play when the party is in full flow.

You will need:

a broomstick for each team

plenty of space

Take the children outside and divide them into teams. Have them run relays while carrying the witches broom. The broom should accompany each team player. First team home wins.

5 Chocolate Countdown

A fast and furiously competitve game best played at top speed by older children.

You will need:

a large bar of chocolate, unwrapped

hats

scarf

gloves

plate

knife and fork

dice

Everyone sits in a circle and takes a turn to roll a dice. The first person to roll a 6 jumps up, puts on the hat, scarf and gloves and then uses the knife and fork to try and cut off a piece of chocolate. For every piece they cut off, they can use their hands to pick it up and eat it. in order to stop the child eating the chocolate the rest of the party children continue to pass the dice around in an attempt to roll a 6. The moment that the 6 is rolled, the first child cutting the chocolate has to stop, take all the extra clothing off and the second child starts to put them on, and so the game goes on until the chocolate is all eaten.

Witch Cake

Flourless Chocolate Cake

Serves 12-20

500 g (1 lb 2 oz) white fondant icing

200 g (7 oz) red fondant icing*

purple edible food colour

100 g (3½ oz) black fondant

120 g (4 ¼ oz) butter

250 g (9 oz) milk compound
chocolate

30 ml (2 tablespoons) Dutch,
unsweetened dark cocoa powder.

9 eggs

330 g (11½ oz) caster (superfine)
sugar

330 g (11½ oz) ground almonds
(almond meal)

50 g (1¾ oz) strawberries,
quartered

50 g (1¾ oz) raspberries

50 g (1¾ oz) blueberries

1 quantity Chocolate Ganache (see
Basic Recipes)

250 g (9 oz) dark compound
chocolate (50% cocoa solids), for
decorating

Make the witch at least one day before you make the cake to allow the fondant to set. Roll out a 30-cm (12in) long and 2–3cm (¾–1¼in) diameter sausage from white fondant and the same from red fondant.

Cut each sausage into 3cm (1¼in) lengths. Place alternate colour cylinders end to end to form two striped sausages for the witch's legs. Use a dab of water to fix the joins. Roll each leg gently to bind the segments together, then bend each leg slightly at the knee to the angle you wish for your witch.

Colour 100 g (3½ oz) white fondant purple. Roll a gumball-sized ball, then roll out to form the base of the hat. Shape the rest of the hat with the rest of the purple fondant as per picture. Join the two pieces using water.

Shape 2 feet using black fondant and attach these to the legs. Allow the fondant to set overnight.

To make the cake, preheat the oven to 180°C/350°F/Gas mark 4. Lightly grease and line 24cm (9½in) cake tin (pan).

Put the butter, milk chocolate and cocoa powder in a bowl and set over a pan of gently simmering water, without allowing the bowl to come into contact with the water and stir. When the mixture is smooth set aside and allow to cool.

In an electric mixer, cream the eggs and sugar until pale. Fold in the ground almonds and melted chocolate mixture.

Pour into the prepared cake tin and bake for 80 minutes, or until the edges come away from the tin and a skewer inserted into the centre comes out clean. Allow to set slightly, then turn out on to a wire rack to go cold.

Cover with ganache. Refrigerate for a couple of hours.

Melt the dark chocoalte in a large bowl set over a pan of gently simmering water. Stir occasionally. Allow to cool for 5 minutes.

Set out sheets of non-stick paper, overlapping them so that they have a combined length of the diameter of the cake. (One long piece of paper is a little harder to handle.) Using a palette knife, spread a thin layer of chocolate across the length of the papers ensuring a good coverage and so that no paper shows through. Cover right to the edges and the bottom, but only to the depth of the cake plus 2 cm (¾ in). Carefully pick up the chocolate-covered paper and wrap it around the cake so that the chocolate faces the cake and the bottom edge of the chocolate-coated paper fits to the bottom of the cake. Allow the chocolate to set for a few hours or until hard. Gently peel away the paper to reveal a paper-effect chocolate shell around the cake.

Place the witch into the cake using the ganache to hold her in place.

*Red fondant is difficult to make so it is readily available pre-coloured. Alternatively you can use red colouring and it will come out pink, which still looks great.

BBQ Bat Wings

Marinated Chicken Wings

Serves 10-12

55 ml (2 fl oz) soy sauce
55 ml (2 fl oz) sweet soy (kecap manis)*
55 ml (2 fl oz) sweet chilli sauce
10-12 chicken wings
oil, for greasing

Mix together the three sauces in a bowl. Toss the chicken wings with the sauce and allow to marinate for 30 minutes to 1 hour.

Preheat the oven to 190°C/375°F/Gas mark 5.

Pour the chicken wings on a lightly greased baking tray and roast in the preheated oven for 10 minutes. Turn the wings and roast for another 5–10 minutes. Once cooked, allow to cool slightly before serving. Serve this dish with napkins.

*Kecap manis is a thick, sweet soy sauce available from Asian supermarkets

Chocolate Broomsticks

Serves 10

300 g (9 oz) solid vegetable
  shortening/Trex or Crisco

100 g (3½ oz) milk compound
  chocolate

2 cups desiccated (dry, unsweetened,
  shredded) coconut

2 cups plain biscuits, crumbed

225g (8 oz / 1 cup) icing
  (confectioners') sugar

1 cup (40 g) Rice Krispies

30 ml (2 tablespoons) unsweetened
  cocoa powder

20 popsticks

Melt the shortening in a large pan over a medium heat.

Stir in the chocolate and allow to melt. Remove from heat and leave to cool for 10 minutes.

Add the remaining ingredients, mix well and leave until cool enough to handle.

Mould broomstick shapes into a bell shape. Place popsticks gently into the top and push all the way in and allow to set for a few hours.

OTHER IDEAS

Cut bat-shaped puff pastry as dippers or mini pizzas.
Serve mini pies/pastries and draw spiders webs on top with tomato ketchup.
Serve boiled eggs as eyeballs by cutting in half.

Gingerbread Houses

Makes 4

150 g (5 oz) butter, chopped

½ cup brown sugar

½ cup treacle

1 teaspoon bicarbonate of soda (baking soda)

1½ tablespoons ground ginger

1 teaspoon ground mixed spice

½ teaspoon baking powder

3½ cups plain (all-purpose) flour

1 egg, lightly beaten

pure icing (confectioners') sugar, for dusting

3 quantities of Royal Icing (see Basic Recipes)

assorted candies or sweets, to decorate

Place butter, sugar and treacle in a saucepan over medium heat. Cook, stirring until sugar has dissolved. Bring to the boil. Remove from heat. Stir in bicarbonate of soda. Transfer to a bowl. Cool for 20 minutes.

Preheat oven to 160°C/325°F/Gas mark 3. Line 2 baking trays with wax paper. Sift ginger, spice, baking powder and flour into a bowl. Add half the flour to the butter mixture and stir well. Add the egg, stirring to combine. Stir in remaining flour until a sticky dough forms. Divide dough in half and shape into discs. Wrap in cling film. Refrigerate for 1 hour.

Roll 1 portion of dough between 2 sheets of wax paper until 5 mm (1/8 in) thick. Cut 20, 7.5 x 8 cm (3 x 3 1/8 in) rectangles from dough, re-rolling scraps. Place on prepared trays, 2 cm (3/4 in) apart. Bake for 8 to 10 minutes or until golden and just firm to touch. Stand on trays for 5 minutes. Cool on a wire rack. Roll remaining dough between 2 sheets wax paper as before. Cut 20, 7 (sides) x 8 cm (base) (2 3/4 x 3 1/8 in) triangles from dough, re-rolling scraps. Place on prepared trays, 2cm apart. Using a 1 x 2 cm (1/3 x 3/4 in) rectangular-shaped cutter, cut a door from half of the triangles. Reserve cutouts and any dough scraps. Bake triangles for 8 to 10 minutes or until golden and just firm to touch. Stand on trays for 5 minutes. Cool on a wire rack.

Place cutout doors on trays. Place on tray, 2 cm (¾ in) apart. Bake for 4 to 5 minutes or until golden and just firm to touch. Stand on trays for 2 minutes. Cool on a wire rack.

To assemble: spread about 2 tablespoons royal icing onto a small cake board or plate to cover. Place 2 triangles (1 with cut-out) on board, about 7 cm apart, pushing into icing to secure. Spoon half the remaining royal icing into a large piping bag fitted with a 3 mm plain nozzle. Pipe icing onto edges of triangles. Attach rectangles to form a roof. Pipe royal icing along edges of house and across top of roof to resemble icicles and snow. Attach doors to house with icing. Repeat with more icing and house pieces. Use royal icing to attach candies for decorating the houses.

This recipe can be used to make gingerbread men. Simply make the same dough recipe, use a gingerbread man cookie cutter to cut out the shapes and follow the cooking instructions above.

Witches' Brew

2 x 340 g (12 oz) packets butter
    cake mix
1 packet green jelly
¼ quantity Buttercream Frosting
    (see Basic Recipes)
red icing paste
10 g (⅓ oz) fondant
1 quantity chocolate Buttercream
    Frosting (see Basic Recipes)

DECORATIONS

1 packet liquorice chocolate logs
5 red liquorice sticks
1 chocolate flake bar, broken
1 marshmallow puff
1 brown Smartie
10cm(4in) piece liquorice strap
2 brown peanut M&Ms
2 red mini frogs
4 sour worms
2 teeth sweets

Preheat oven to 180°C/350°F/Gas mark 4 and butter and line the cake tin.

Prepare packets of cake mix, following directions on packet, and pour into a pudding basin tin 19.5cm (7¾in) in diametre, 5.5cm (2in) deep. Bake for 30 minutes, cover with foil and bake for another 30 minutes. Test with a skewer to make sure the cake is cooked. Leave to cool for 10 minutes, then turn onto a cooling rack.

Meanwhile, prepare the jelly following directions on packet and refrigerate to set.

While cakes cool, colour the butter frosting red and colour the fondant pale pink.

Hollow out the top third of the cake. Using a palette knife, frost the cake with the chocolate icing. Spread the red frosting onto the base of the cake.

Arrange the liquorice logs, red liquorice sticks and flake bar at the base to resemble logs. Spoon the jelly into the cake. Mould the fondant to look like a hand. Attach the marshmallow to the Smartie with icing to make an eye. Use liquorice and M&Ms to make spiders. Add remaining decorations to jelly.

Clown
Parties

Clown Parties

Roll up, roll up. This crazy theme works for a whole host of ages but is probably best suited to the under sixes. Make it visually stimulating with a bold and bright colour scheme. This theme works well for boys and girls

Ideal age group: 1–6 years

Decorations

Big bright and loud is the way to go with this theme. Start with lots of balloons in as many different and bright colours as you like to give the space a circus theme. Add streamers and drape red and white material from the ceiling to give the space that circus feel. You could even use bright flags and banners throughout the space.

When dressing the room, use solid colour. A bright tablecloth paired with bright plates and cups will add that crazy circus theme to the party. Red and white stripy popcorn boxes filled with flowers and lollies will also make for fun table settings.

If you've got the budget you could even hire some fun fair crazy mirrors and place them around the space. Or a candy floss or popcorn machine could be hired to provide an authentic circus feel. A petting zoo could be hired to come to the party. These will include lots of great animals for the children to interact with, just make sure you have plenty of space.

Check
- Balloons, balloons, balloons
- Red and white streamers
- Bright tablecloths, plates and cutlery
- Red and white popcorn boxes filled with flowers and lollies
- Crazy mirrors
- Candy floss sticks and stand
- Petting zoo

Activities

There are lots of silly activities that can be played within the circus theme. Remember that you can adapt many old party games to work with your theme.

1 Crazy Cream

This game takes the classic cream pie in the clowns face and takes it a step further. The children will love becoming the custard cream clowns in this game and are sure to enjoy a true taste of the circus.

You will need:

plates
whipped cream or similar
prizes

Begin by filling the plates with whipped cream. Bury the prizes in the whipped cream. With their hands behind their backs, the children must place their faces into the cream and try to pull out a prize using only their teeth. To add an additional element give the children a time limit (60 seconds is enough). You could add food colouring to each of the plates of cream to give the cream some fun colours.

2 Bottle Toss

At the fairground there are always plenty of fun games to play. Why not bring this one to your party so the children can step right up and win themselves a fantastic prize?

You will need:

ten empty plastic bottles
three bean bags, or similar
felt-tipped pen

Draw a star on the bottom of three plastic bottles. Arrange the plastic bottles in a line. The idea of the game is for the children to throw the bean bags at the plastic bottles and knock them over. If the child knock over a plastic bottle with a star on the bottom, they are a winner.

To make this game a little bit more challenging, you can fill the bottles with coloured water. This will give them a little extra weight and will make it a harder for the children to knock them down—just remember to put the lids back on to avoid mess.

3 Three-legged Race

Clowns really are uncoordinated. How coordinated will the children be when one of their legs is tied to another child's and they are in a race? This game is sure to deliver plenty of laughs.

You will need:

scarves—one for every two children

This game is just like any other race, except here the children have to work in pairs in order to win! Organise the children into pairs and have them stand side by side. Using the scarf, tie middle two legs of the children together. Establish a start and finish line for the race. On your marks, get set, go! The team to go over the finish line first are the winners.

REMEMBER...

Safety first. always make sure that the children understand how to play the game and that they are safe throughout.

4 Hoopla

A traditional fairground game that tests skill.

You will need:

a basket
plenty of bean bags or similar light object to throw

Have the children stand an equal distance around a large basket. Give each child three bean bags. The aim is to throw the bean bags and get them in the basket. The children should take turns and begin standing quite close to the basket so that they all have more chance of getting the maximum number of bean bags into the target. Once everyone has had a turn, each player takes a step backwards and the game begins again. The aim is to see who can hit the target the greatest number of times from the furthest distance. If a child misses each of their three shots then they are out of the game.

5 The Tray Game

A quiet game to keep children guessing and to test the memory.

You will need:

a tray
at least 10 small theme-related objects that will all fit on the tray
a kitchen towel
paper and pencil for each child

Fill the tray with 10 small objects such as a juggling ball, a lollipop, a red clown's nose, a balloon, a felt-tipped pen, a small coin, a sweet, etc. Cover the tray and place it in the centre of the children. Explain to them that on the tray are a number of objects, then hold each item up in turn and name it. Tell the children that they have a few minutes to look at the objects and try and commit them to memory. When everyone is satisfied that they have looked for long enough, cover the tray with the kitchen towel and remove it from the room. Now ask the children to write down as many of the items as they can remember. It's harder than they might think. The one who remembers the most items wins.

Clown Cake

This is the same cake and method as the Fairy Cake.

Makes 1

250 g (9 oz) unsalted butter

250 g (9 oz) caster (superfine) sugar

15 ml (1 tablespoon) vanilla extract

10 eggs, beaten

175 g (6 oz) plain (all-purpose) flour, sifted

500 g (18 oz) self-raising (self-rising) flour, sifted

40 ml (1½ fl oz) milk

200 ml (7 fl oz) buttermilk

red, blue, green and yellow edible food colour

2 quantities Buttercream Frosting (see Basic Recipes)

100 g (3½ oz) red fondant

50 g (1¾ oz) black fondant

30 g (1 oz) purple fondant

100 g (3½ oz) white fondant

rose or pistachio-flavoured Persian fairy floss

Preheat the oven to 160°C/325°F/Gas mark 3. Lightly grease and line one 24 cm (9½ in) large cake tin (pan).

Beat the butter in an electric mixer until pale and creamy, about 5–7 minutes. Slowly add the caster sugar, then the vanilla extract until the sugar is combined. Add the eggs one at a time. Scrape down the bowl occasionally. Add the flours, milk and buttermilk and mix by hand.

Divide the batter into six even portions in six bowls. Add a colour of the rainbow to each—red, oranged (combine red and yellow), yellow, green, blue, and, violet (combine blue and red). Place 45 ml (3 tablespoons) of the first colour in the centre of the cake tin. Put the same amount of the next colour in the middle of the first batter and allow the new cake batter to spread the first one. Continue with the rest of the colours until all the batter is used up. Don't spread the batter with a spatula; the batter will spread by itself.

Bake for 45–60 minutes or until a skewer comes out clean when inserted into the centre of the cake. Leave to set for 10 minutes, before turning out on to a wire rack to cool.

Cover the cake with buttercream. Roll out some red fondant to make a mouth and big nose and place onto the cake. Make some eyes and makeup, as per the picture or design your own. Use pink or green fairy floss for the hair.

Candy Apples

Apple Cake Pops

Makes 20-30 pops

CAKE

2 large cooking apples, peeled and
    diced
150 g (5 oz) caster (superfine)
    sugar
75 g (3 oz) butter, melted
1 egg
115 g (4 oz) self-raising (self-rising)
    flour
5 ml (1 teaspoon) ground cinnamon
5 ml (1 teaspoon) baking powder
20 g (^{2}/$_3$ oz) plain biscuits,
    crumbled
50 g (1^3/$_4$ oz) white chocolate,
    melted
12-20 popsticks

Preheat the oven to 180°C/350°F/Gas mark 4. Lightly grease and line a 24 cm (9½ in) tin.

To make the cake, put the diced apples and 50 g (1¾ oz) sugar in a saucepan and heat over low heat until the apples are stewed and soft. Allow to cool.

In a mixing bowl combine the butter and rest of the sugar and beat until light and fluffy. Stir in the egg. Sift over the flour with the cinnamon and baking powder and stir to combine. Finally, add the apple sauce to the mix and stir well.

Pour into the prepared cake tin and bake in the preheated oven for 30–40 minutes, or until a skewer comes out clean when inserted into the centre.

Leave to set for 10 minutes, then turn out on to a wire rack to go cold.

Crumble the cake into a mixing bowl, add the biscuit, mix to combine, and form small balls using your hands. You want a fairly sticky mix, which won't fall apart. Make the balls quite small as they can get too heavy for the popsticks. Using a little white chocolate, attach the popsticks to the balls and refrigerate for a few hours. (This step is a good one if the kids want to help.)

(Continued over the page.)

CANDY

400 g (14 oz) caster (superfine)
    sugar
180 ml (6 fl oz) water
120 ml (4 fl oz) golden (corn) syrup
2.5 ml (½ teaspoon) red food
    colouring
Note: there are melting candy
    products available in different
    colours and you may find those
    products easier to work with if you
    can source them

To make the candy, (on the day of eating)
put the sugar and the water in a large pan over
a medium heat and stir until the sugar dissolves.
Add the golden syrup and a few drops of red food
colouring, stir to combine, then bring to the boil.
Be careful as the sugar is very hot and may spit
when stirred.

Using a pastry brush and some water carefully
brush the sides of the pan occasionally to avoid
sugar crystallising on the pan. After 5 minutes
turn the heat down to a simmer and continue to
cook for about 20 minutes until the temperature
reaches 250°C (500°F) on a sugar thermometre.
Allow to cool for 1 minute.

Line a tray with non-stick paper (baking
parchment). Dip the apple balls into the candy
and allow the excess to drip off. Set on the baking
tray to harden. Work quickly before your candy
becomes too thick.

Chicken Popcorn

Makes 20

500 g (17½ oz) chicken tenderloins
   (use breast if unavailable)
½ cup plain (all-purpose) flour
3 eggs beaten
1 cup fine breadcrumbs

Preheat oven to 200°C/400°F/Gas mark 6. Line a large baking tray with non-stick paper.

Cut the tenderloins into 20 bite-sized pieces.

Roll each piece of chicken in the flour, ensuring they are completely covered in flour. Shake off excess flour. Now coat each piece in the egg, ensuring they are covered in egg. Allow excess egg to drip off. Roll the chicken pieces in the breadcrumbs, ensuring even coverage. Shake off excess breadcrumbs and spread evenly onto the baking tray. Place into the oven and cook for 20 minutes or until golden and cooked through. (Alternatively, you can deep-fry in medium hot oil for 3-5 minutes or until golden). Allow to cool slightly before serving.

Popcorn Sticks

Makes 12

450 g (15 oz) caster (superfine)
    sugar
90 ml (3 fl oz) water
20 g (²/₃ oz) unsalted butter
300 g (10½ oz) popping corn
20 popsticks

Put the water and sugar in a saucepan. Heat gently until the sugar dissolves, then boil for 3–4 minutes. washing down the sides with a pastry brush dipped in water to avoid sugar crystallising, until it turns caramel.

Remove from heat and stir in the butter. Mix in the popcorn.

Allow to cool a few minutes until it is cool enough to handle, but still malleable. Mould the popcorn around the popsticks and insert the sticks into a block of styrofoam to set.

OTHER IDEAS
Serve fairy floss, mini hamburgers and lemonade in glass bottles for a circus feel.
Use a melon baller to shape watermelon into 'clown noses'.
Cook farfalle pasta and colour into 'clown bowties'.
Use the 'broomsticks' recipe and add coloured candies for rainbow crispies.

Jelly Bites

Makes 20

1 packet green jelly crystals
1 packet orange jelly crystals
1 packet red jelly crystals
Note: You can use colours to suit
   your party theme.

You will also need 3 ice cube trays.

Mix each of the jelly colours in a different bowl as per packet instructions. Allow to cool to room temperature. Fill each of the ice cube holes one-third of the way with the red jelly. Place in the fridge and allow to set for 3–4 hours. Repeat with the remaining colours. When fully set, turn out and serve.

Clown Cupcakes

Makes 18

200 g (7 oz) soft unsalted butter

1¾ cups caster (superfine) sugar

2 teaspoons vanilla extract

4 large eggs, at room temperature

2¾ cups self-raising (self-rising) flour

1 cup milk

500 g (17½ oz) ice cream

18 waffle ice cream cones

confectionary, for decorating

Preheat oven to 180°C/350°F/Gas mark 4. Line an 18-hole muffin or cupcake pan with paper cases.

Place the butter and sugar in a clean bowl or stand mixer, and beat on high until light and fluffy. Turn down to a medium speed, add the vanilla. Add the eggs slowly one at a time. Sift in the flour and fold in gently using a metal spoon. Fold in the milk.

Spoon the mixture into the paper cases.

Place in the oven for 15–20 minutes. When they are ready they should be golden brown, and when pressed gently on top, spring back.

Transfer to a wire rack to cool completely.

Cut a small cone shape out of the tops of each cupcake (for the ice cream to sit in slightly). Use an ice cream scoop to scoop 18 nice round balls from the ice cream. Place on top of cupcakes. Use lollies for the eyes and nose, and place a 'collar' of lollies around the base of the ice cream ball. Place an ice cream cone on top and freeze until ready to serve.

Hotdogs

Chorizo, Caramelised Onion and Tomato Relish Pockets

Makes 12

2 tablespoons olive oil

4 onions, sliced

45 ml (3 tablespoons) balsamic
  vinegar

60 ml (4 tablespoons) light
  brown sugar

15 ml (1 tablespoon) seeded
  mustard

5 ml (1 teaspoon) mustard seeds

5 ml (1 teaspoon) ground cumin

5 ml (1 teaspoon) ground
  coriander (cilantro)

5 ml (1 teaspoon) ground turmeric

450 g (1 lb) can chopped
  tomatoes

50 g (1¾ oz) roasted red bell
  peppers (capsicums)

6 chorizo sausages

1 packet flat bread

salt and pepper

lettuce, to serve

3 large tomatoes, sliced, to serve

To caramelise the onions, warm 1 tablespoon olive oil in a large saucepan over medium heat. Add ¾ of the onions and cook until soft and translucent. Increase the heat and add 30 ml (2 tablespoons) of the balsamic vinegar. Stir to coat the onions. Add 45 ml (3 tablespoons) of brown sugar and cook until the liquid has thickened and onions are caramelised.

To make the tomato relish, in another saucepan, fry the remaining onion in 1 tablespoon of olive oil on medium heat until soft then add the mustard and mustard seeds. Put a lid over the saucepan and allow the mustard seeds to 'pop' for a minute or two. Add the remaining balsamic vinegar and brown sugar to the pan, stirring to coat the onions.

Add the dried spices, stir well and then add the canned tomatoes. Season with salt and pepper.

Finely dice the roasted bell peppers, add them to the tomato relish and cook on low to medium heat for 10–20 minutes until the sauce is thick, and stirring occasionally so it doesn't catch on the base of the pan.

Cut the chorizo sausages in half lengthways and fry on each side in a hot frying pan with oil until browned on both sides.

Place a sausage half on a flat bread, and add some lettuce and fresh tomato and roll up. You can tie the hotdogs with some cooking twine/string and wrap with some circus-themed paper. (You can print a simple red and white striped pattern on your computer.)

Under the Sea Parties

Under the Sea Parties

The deep dark sea is a mysterious place, full of wonder and magic. This theme can bring mermaids, pirates and sea monsters altogether. This theme can be tailored to appeal to boys and girls of mixed ages. Or simply pick one of the themes to work with your party.

Ideal age group: 2+ years

Decorations

Greens, blues, yellows and whites are delightful colour choices for this theme. Placing fake seaweed and fishing nets around the space will help to give an underwater feel to the party. You can also use fake anchors to depict the bottom of the ocean bed.

Use a fishing net as a tablecloth. Place goldfish bowls as table decorations with toy fish in them. You might even want to add food colouring to some of the fish bowls to give them sea water colour. (Don't do this if you have a real gold fish to place on the table!)

Use blue and white material around the outskirts of the space to give an impression of waves washing up on the beach.

Make your own starfish by using a star stencil to draw and cut stars from cardboard. Make the points of the stars curved and paint the shapes yellow, Once they're dry, stick or hang them around the space and put them on the table.

If you've got space you could buy a few bags of sandpit sand, and use it for an 'ocean bed' floor. Messy but very effective.

Activities

Under the Sea is such an expansive theme that there really are plenty of games and themes to draw ideas and inspiration from. You can link many of the activities back to mermaids, pirates or even sea monsters and take the children on a wonderful deep sea adventure.

1 Brilliant Bubbles

Deep under the ocean there are lots of air bubbles that need popping. It's not just fish that love to pop bubbles, kids love it too. The children will have a crazy time trying to pop bubbles in all kinds of ways, using all kinds of parts of their bodies. Make one placemat for each child (see Decorations for instructions).

You will need:
bubble machine or bubble wand
starfish placemats

The aim of this game is for the children to pop as many bubbles as possible within a given time limit. Easy I hear you say. Well, to make this game even more challenging, the children are not allowed to use their hands. They can only pop the bubbles using the parts of the body that you call out. For example, with their noses, chins, bottoms and tummies. They must remain standing on their starfish placemats and not fall off trying to pop those bubbles.

2 Seaweed Tug of War

If the children are to beat the sea monsters and rule the Seven Seas, they will need to have big strong muscles. This fun game is perfect to play with a large group of children and is sure to be a hit.

You will need:
a long rope

Found at the bottom of the ocean, this long piece of 'seaweed' is ideal for the children to use to test their strength. Divide the children into two teams, making sure you have equal numbers on each team. The aim of the game is for the two teams to pull against each other using the rope. The team that can pull the opposite team over a pre-set mark first are the winners.

3 Sticky Starfish

Under the sea there are plenty of starfish. However, sometimes because of the seaweed the starfish can become stuck. It's the children's job to try and save the starfish from the seaweed.

You will need:

lots of energy

In its simplest form this is a game of tag with a deep-sea twist. One player is selected to be the 'seaweed' and the rest are starfish. The seaweed has to catch a starfish and tag it by tapping on the shoulder. A tagged starfish must stand in a starfish shape until one of the other starfish untags the stuck starfish by crawling through his or her legs. The aim of the game is for the seaweed to 'stick' all the starfish and for the starfishes to stop them. If there are a lot of children playing you can increase the number of children playing as the seaweed.

Starfish Cake

Lemon Delicious Cake

Makes 1

400 g (14 oz) plain (all-purpose)
    flour
20 ml (4 teaspoons) baking powder
400 g (14 oz) caster (superfine)
    sugar
8 eggs
300 ml (10 fl oz) sour cream
zest and juice of 2 lemons
300 ml (10 fl oz) vegetable oil
1 quantity Buttercream
250 g (9 oz) plain biscuits, finely
    crushed
100 g (3 ½ oz) white fondant
50g (1 ¾ oz) dark chocolate,
    melted, or writing icing

LEMON CURD

3 large egg yolks
120 ml (4 fl oz) fresh lemon juice
200 g (7 oz) caster (superfine)
    sugar
100 g (3 ½ oz) cold butter, cubed

Preheat the oven to 180°C/350°F/Gas mark 4. Lightly grease and line two 24cm (9 ½in) square cake tins (pans).

Sift the flour and baking powder into a large mixing bowl, then stir in the sugar.

In another bowl, whisk the eggs, sour cream, lemon zest, 120 ml (4 fl oz) lemon juice and the vegetable oil together until smooth.

Add the flour/sugar mixture and fold in until just combined.

Divide the mixture between the prepared cake tins and bake for 30–45 minutes, or until the sides come away from the cake tin and a skewer inserted into the centre comes out clean.

Leave cakes to stand for 10 minutes, then turn out on to a wire rack to go cold.

Cut a star shape from each cake.

To make the lemon curd, put the egg yolks, lemon juice and sugar in a metal bowl and set over a saucepan of gently simmering water. Ensure the water doesn't touch the base of the bowl. Stir well to dissolve the sugar and keep stirring so that the eggs don't overcook and to ensure that the curd is smooth.

When the mixture is thick enough to coat the back of a spoon, the curd is ready. If you get small lumps, strain the curd through a fine strainer.

Remove from the heat and add the butter one cube at a time. Whisk lightly to dissolve, before adding the next cube until all the butter is incorporated. Decant into a glass or ceramic bowl, cover and allow to set overnight.

Mix the buttercream with the lemon curd and spread a quantity over the top of one cake. Stack the other cake on top, then cover the cake with icing. (See Superhero Cake for method to cover a cut cake.) Sprinkle with the crushed biscuits for a sandy effect. Decorate with a few chocolate seashells around the cake, if you have them.

Roll out some fondant eyes and pipe melted chocolate for pupils and a mouth.

Whale Tail Pizzas
Octopus Hotdogs

Makes 12-30

WHALE TAIL PIZZAS

1 teaspoon olive oil

1 onion, finely chopped

1 clove garlic, minced

425 g (15 oz) tin pureed tomatoes

1 tablespoon tomato paste

salt to taste

1 teaspoon sugar

3 sheets (about 500 g/17½ oz)
   puff pastry

1 egg, beaten

100 g (3½ oz) grated cheese

OCTOPUS HOTDOGS

30 cocktail sausages/frankfurts*

WHALE TAIL PIZZAS
For sauce, heat the oil over a medium heat in a saucepan and fry the onion and garlic. Add the tomatoes and tomato paste and simmer for 10–15 minutes. Add some salt and the sugar and cook for a further 5 minutes. Allow to cool.

Preheat the oven to 190°C/375°F/Gas mark 6. To make the whale tails, cut whale tail shapes from puff pastry using the template on the following page. Prick the pastry all over with a fork, brush with beaten egg and bake for 15 minutes until golden. Top with the pizza sauce and some cheese and when you're ready to serve, bake for another 5 minutes until the cheese melts. Add other traditional pizza toppings, such as ham, if you like.

OCTOPUS HOTDOGS
To make the octopus hotdogs, cut slits two-thirds of the way up each cocktail sausage to make 8 legs.

Drop the sausages into boiling water for 60 seconds. Once cooked, remove and allow to cool slightly before serving.

*Use a better-quality sausage if you think the kids will like it, ones with a natural casing are better than synthetic ones as they curl better for the legs.

Whale Tail template

pastry cutting guide

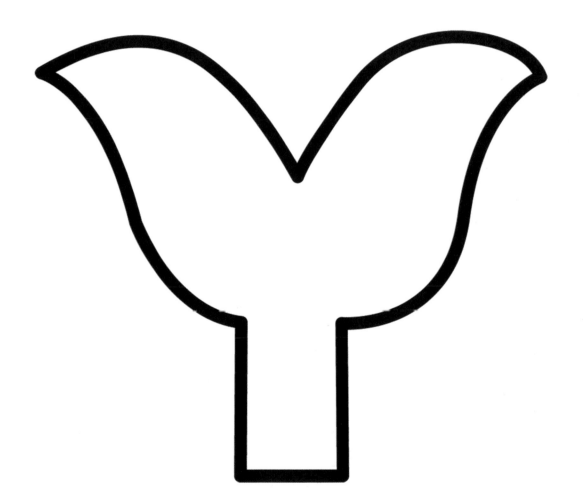

Sushi Rolls

Serves 8-12

4 cups water

400g (14 oz) arborio or sushi rice

30 ml (2 tablespoons) mirin
(Japanese sweet rice vinegar)

8-10 large green (uncooked) shrimp
(prawn) cutlets*

1 large cucumber

1 large avocado

45ml (3 tablespoons) mayonnaise

1 packet seaweed paper*

soy sauce, to serve

salt and pepper

Note: This will make 4 rolls which
can be cut into 6-8 pieces

Put the water and rice in a large pan, bring to the boil then allow to simmer until all the water has been absorbed, 10–15 minutes. Cover and let steam for 5 minutes. Add the mirin to the pan and set aside to cool for 30 minutes.

Meanwhile, skewer each prawn through the tail to the head to keep them relatively straight while cooking. Cook each prawn for 1 minute on each side in a hot frying pan, with some oil. Season to taste. Leave to cool, then remove the skewers.

Slice the cucumber and avocado into long, thin batons.

Set out a sushi mat and place a seaweed paper on top with the shiny side down and the longest side going left to right.

Arrange a thin layer of rice over the entire paper except for a 2 cm (¾ in) strip at the top.

Put a thin strip of prawns (you may need to cut them and leave the tails over the edge on both sides), avocado and cucumber down the centre of the rice along the longest length and finish with a small strip of mayonnaise.

Starting at the side closest to you, roll the bamboo mat upwards and away from you, holding the mat firmly but gently until the rice edges meet. Dip your finger in a little water and dab the 2 cm (¾ in) strip with no rice to help the paper stick. Release the mat and continue rolling and seal the roll.

Refrigerate the rolls for 1 hour; this will make them easier to cut. Using a sharp knife (not a serrated knife) very gently cut each roll into pieces. Serve at room temperature with soy sauce.

*You can also use sushi-grade salmon or tuna in place of the prawn for a seafood theme.

Clam Cakes with Lemon Curd

Makes 12

70 g (2 ½ oz) butter, melted, plus
    extra for greasing
3 eggs
100 g (3 ½ oz) caster (superfine)
    sugar
grated zest of 1 lime
180 g (6 oz) plain (all-purpose) flour
1.5 ml (¼ teaspoon) baking powder

LEMON CURD
3 large egg yolks
120 ml (4 fl oz) fresh lemon juice
200 g (7 oz) caster (superfine)
    sugar
100 g (3 ½ oz) cold butter, cubed
50 g (1 ¾ oz) milk compound
    chocolate, melted

Preheat the oven to 200°C/400°F/Gas mark 6. Lightly grease a madeleine pan with butter.

Put the eggs, sugar and grated lime zest in a mixing bowl and beat with an electric beater until pale and creamy. Sift in the flour, baking powder and butter and beat well. Fill the madeleine pan with batter and bake for 15–20 minutes until golden. Allow to cool slightly and turn out on to a wire rack.

To make the lemon curd, put the egg yolks, lemon juice and sugar in a metal bowl and set over a saucepan of gently simmering water. Ensure the water doesn't touch the base of the bowl. Stir well to dissolve the sugar and keep stirring so that the eggs don't overcook and to ensure that the curd is smooth.

When the mixture is thick enough to coat the back of a spoon, the curd is ready. To remove small lumps, strain the curd through a fine strainer.

Remove from the heat and add the butter one cube at a time. Whisk lightly to dissolve, before adding the next cube until all the butter is incorporated. Decant into a glass or ceramic bowl, cover and allow to set overnight.

Use the lemon curd to stick two madeleines together to form a clam.

Pour the melted chocolate into a piping tube fitted with a fine writing nozzle. Pipe eyes on the clams. You could hide an edible pearl in the clam, or make small pearls from yoghurt-covered raisins, if you like.

OTHER IDEAS
Use 'snail' bread recipe to make turtles.
Carve a whole watermelon into a shark.
Seahorse-shaped cookies.

Starfish Pies

Makes 24

500-700 g (17½ -1 lb 9 oz) ready-
   rolled shortcrust pastry
1 egg, beaten
350-400 g (12-14 oz) smoked cod
150 g (5 oz) clean, white fish,
   skinned and deboned
1 cup milk
1 bay leaf
60 g (2 oz) leek, chopped
1 teaspoon olive oil
30 g (1 oz) butter
2 tablespoons plain (all-purpose) flour
½ cup cream
salt and pepper, to taste

Preheat the oven to 180°C/350°F/Gas mark 4.

Grease a 24-hole mini muffin pan. Line each hole with some pastry, trimming the edges, but allowing the pastry to come up higher than the edge, to make 24 pie cases. Brush with some egg and cook for 10–15 minutes or until golden

Place all the fish in a deep saucepan with the milk and a bay leaf, bring to the boil, then turn down to simmer and poach the fish for 3–5 minutes. Strain the liquid from the fish and reserve both. Flake the fish into small pieces.

In another saucepan over medium heat, lightly fry the leek in the oil. When soft, add the butter and stir until melted. Add the flour and mix to form a paste. Add the poaching liquid and the cream and stir until smooth. Add the fish and cook on a low heat for a further 10–15 minutes, adding salt and pepper to taste. Once cool, fill the cases with the cod mix and use the trimmings of the pastry to cut star-shaped tops. Brush with some egg. When you're ready to serve, place into the oven for 10 minutes or until golden.

Fish Bites

Serves 10-15

80 ml (3 fl oz) sweet soy sauce
  (kecap manis)
80 ml (3 fl oz) sweet chilli sauce
30 ml (2 tablespoons) soy sauce
zest and juice of 1 lemon
30 g (1 oz) coriander, chopped
30 g (1 oz) mint leaves, chopped
400 g (14 oz) white fish fillets,
  skinned and boned
1 small carrot
30 ml (2 tablespoons) green or red
  Thai curry paste
½ cup breadcrumbs
500 ml (17½ fl oz) oil for frying

For the sauce, combine the sweet soy, sweet chilli and soy sauce with the lemon juice, half the coriander leaves and half the mint leaves in a blender or food processor. Set aside in the refrigerator until ready to serve.

Combine the fish, carrot, remaining coriander and mint leaves, curry paste, breadcrumbs, lemon zest and a 15 ml (1 tablespoon) of the sauce in a food processor. The mixture should be dry enough to roll into balls. If yours is too wet, add more breadcrumbs.

Roll the mixture into bite-sized balls. When you're ready to serve them, deep-fry them in hot oil, turning them to cook evenly for 2–3 minutes.

Serve in sea-themed boxes or paper cones with some dipping sauce.

Fish Fingers

Makes 18

600 g (21 oz) firm white fish such
    as ling (if unavailable, ask your
    fishmonger)
½ cup plain (all-purpose) flour
3 eggs, lightly beaten
2 cups fine breadcrumbs
salt and pepper to taste
½ cup mayonnaise or aioli, to serve

Preheat oven to 200°C/400°F/Gas mark 6. Line two baking trays with non-stick paper.

Cut the fish into thin strips about 8–10 cm (3–4 in) long.

Coat each piece firstly in flour, shaking off excess flour. Next, coat in the beaten egg, ensuring the whole piece is covered, allowing excess egg to drip off. Finally coat in breadcrumbs mixed with salt and pepper. Place on the baking trays. Bake in the oven until golden and cooked through—about 15 minutes.

Mini Pasties

Makes 24

3 medium potatoes, peeled and
   chopped
1 small carrot, peeled
1 small onion, peeled
¼ cup peas, cooked
¼ cup corn, cooked
salt and pepper
6 sheets (1 kg/2 lb 4 oz) puff pastry,
   nearly thawed
1 egg, beaten

Preheat oven to 200°C/400°F/Gas mark 6. Line 2 baking trays with non-stick baking paper.

Place the potatoes into a saucepan of water and bring to the boil. Cook until potatoes are soft. Drain and mash. Place the carrot and onion in a food processor and pulse until fine. Add the minced vegetable to the mashed potatoes, along with the peas, corn, salt and pepper.

Cut 24 10-cm (4 in) rounds from the pastry sheets. Place a tablespoon of the mixture in the centre of each circle. Fold the pastry in half over the mixture and pinch the ends to seal. Place onto the baking trays.

Brush with a little egg and bake for 20–25 minutes or until golden. Allow to cool slightly before serving.

Seasonal
Parties

Seasonal Parties

Christmas, New Year and Easter are just a few of the many special occasions that can be celebrated with a party. As well as organising a great party for the adults, don't forget to make sure that the kids have a great time too.

Decorations

It is usually easy to find inexpensive decorations for seasonal celebrations. Most shops and supermarkets stock plenty of items, though if you are feeling particularly creative here are a few ideas you might like to try.

For Easter, purchase small baskets and fill them with brightly coloured eggs. Hard-boil several eggs, then place them into cold water for one hour. Then fill several containers with water, and add 1 teaspoon of vinegar for each cup of water used. Add as many drops of food colour as you like, until each container is the desired colour. Add the eggs to the coloured vinegar water and leave for a few minutes for them to absorb the colour. Remove the eggs from the dye and dry off. Brush with olive or vegetable oil and leave to dry.

For Christmas, why not create a personalised wreath for the front door? It's really easy, and fantastic fun! Ask each family member to draw an outline of their hand on a piece of cardboard. Cut out each hand print and paint them using festive colours. Once the hand prints are dry, glue the forefinger of each hand to the palm of the following hand until all of the hands are glued together in a circle.

Check
- Brightly coloured boiled eggs
- Personalised Christmas wreath

Activities

There are plenty of activities that are specific to different seasons and holidays. Here are just a few:

Easter Egg Hunt

This game will have the children searching high and low for their Easter eggs. It's a fabulous way to give the children their eggs.

You will need:

Easter eggs

Before the children arrive at the party, go around the party space hiding lots of small and large Easter eggs. When the children arrive, explain to them that the Easter Bunny just came hopping through and in his rush dropped lots of eggs. You can then send them out to claim their loot.

To add a twist to this classic game, why not come up with some cryptic clues that the children must follow and solve to find the the grand prize (all the eggs together).

Christmas gingerbread men decorating

This fun, creative and yummy activity is sure to be a hit not only with the little kids, but the 'big' kids too.

You will need:

plain gingerbread men
piping bags filled with icing
sweets

If you are confident in the kitchen, why not whip up some yummy gingerbread men ready for the party, but hold off decorating them? If you are not so confident or are short of time, you could ask your local baker's shop to make you a batch of PLAIN gingerbread men.

Remember..

Egg-based icing will not keep for long, so make it on the day of the party or the day before.'

Fill the piping bags with your chosen icing and simply have fun decorating the cookies. Use the icing as 'glue', and stick on your chosen sweets, creating a very festive character. Once you're finished, you can eat your creations. Yummy!

These recipes are easily interchangeable between Easter and Christmas.

For Halloween you can also use ideas from the witch/wizard theme.

Easter Simnel or Christmas Cake

Serves 10-12

400 g (14 oz) crushed pineapple

200 g (7 oz) glacé cherries

400 g (14 oz) mixed dried fruit

2.5 ml (½ teaspoon) ground
  nutmeg

2.5 ml (½ teaspoon) ground
  cinnamon

2.5 ml (½ teaspoon) ground allspice
  (apple pie spice)

250 g (9 oz) light brown sugar,
  packed

125 g (4½ oz) unsalted butter

80 g (3 oz) flaked (sliced) almonds
  (optional)

30 ml (2 tablespoons) brandy or
  sherry (optional)

250 g (9 oz) self-raising (self-rising)
  flour

250 g (9 oz) plain (all-purpose)
  flour

2 eggs, beaten

500 g (17½ oz) marzipan, for
  Easter version

20 g (²/3 oz) apricot jam, for Easter

Preheat the oven to 160°C/325°F/Gas mark 3.

Put all the fruit, the spices, sugar, butter, almonds and brandy or sherry in a large pan over a medium heat. Bring to the boil and boil for 5 minutes.

Sift the flours into a bowl, mix in the boiled fruit, then add the eggs.

FOR CHRISTMAS
Pour the batter into a lightly greased and lined log tin (20 x 8 cm/7¾ x 3 in). You can also use two half round pans and sandwich them together using apricot jam. Bake for 1 hour or until a skewer comes out clean. Leave the cake to set in the tin. When cool, turn out on to a wire rack to go completely cold. Drizzle with glacé icing and decorate with fresh holly sprigs, or make your own from fondant icing.

FOR EASTER
Bake in a lightly greased 24 cm (9½ in) round cake tin (pan) for about an hour or until skewer comes out clean.

Leave the cake to set in the tin. When cool, turn out on to a wire rack to go completely cold. Cut the top off the cake to create a flat surface with straight edges.

GLACÉ ICING FOR CHRISTMAS

250 g (9 oz) icing (confectioners')
    sugar
20 ml (4 teaspoons) boiling water
15g (½ oz) butter, melted

Brush the top with a little apricot jam heated in a small pan, to help seal the marzipan to the cake.

Roll a disc of marzipan and place on top of the cake, trimming the edges to fit.

Roll 11 small balls of marzipan and fix them around the cake, securing them by dabbing with a little water. Place the cake under a hot grill to slightly brown the marzipan.

GLACÉ ICING
Dissolve the icing sugar in the water, then stir in the butter.

Festive Cookies

240 g (8 ½ oz) cold butter, cubed

115 g (4 oz) icing (confectioners')
   sugar, plus extra for dusting

10 ml (2 teaspoons) vanilla extract

400 g (14 oz) plain (all-purpose)
   flour

4 egg yolks

1 quantity Royal Icing and edible
   decorations

Preheat the oven to 160°C/325°F/Gas mark 3.

Put the butter and icing sugar in an electric mixer and beat until creamy.

Add the vanilla extract, then the flour and the egg yolks. Mix until the dough forms a ball.

Knead the dough by hand for a few seconds, then roll out on a work surface lightly dusted with icing sugar to a sheet 1 cm (3/8 in) thick. Stamp out shapes using your choice of cookie cutter.

Place on a tray lined with non-stick baking paper and bake for about 30 minutes, or until golden.

Leave to set for a few minutes, before turning out on to a wire rack to go cold.

Decorate with frosting and any other decorations of choice, when cold.

Chocolate Brownie Cupcakes

Makes 18

250 g (9 oz) butter

200 g (7 oz) dark (bittersweet)
  chocolate

30 ml (2 tablespoons) Dutch cocoa

300 g (10½ oz) caster (superfine)
  sugar

4 eggs

150 g (5 oz) plain (all-purpose)
  flour, sifted

50 g (1¾ oz) ground almonds
  (almond meal)

1 quantity Chocolate Ganache (see
  Basic Recipes)

18 strawberries (Christmas)

1 quantity Royal Icing (Christmas)
  (see Basic Recipes)

36 mini Easter eggs (Easter)

50–100 g (1¾ – 3½ oz) chocolate
  shavings (Easter)

Preheat the oven to 180°C/350°F/Gas mark 4.
Line three 6-hole cupcake trays with paper cases.

Melt the butter and the chocolate in a large
heatproof bowl set over a pan of gently simmering
water.

Stir in the cocoa and allow to cool.

Place the caster sugar, eggs, flour, and ground
almonds into a stand mixer. Add the chocolate
mixture and stir to combine.

Pour into cupcake cases and bake for 30
minutes. Test to see if they are cooked through
by gently pressing the centre with a finger. If the
sponge bounces back, the cakes are baked.

Leave to stand in the cupcake tray for 10
minutes, then turn out onto a wire rack to go cold.

Top each with a swirl of Chocolate Ganache.

FOR CHRISTMAS
Pipe a small disc of icing onto the top of each
cupcake. Top with a strawberry for a Santa
hat and pipe a small bauble onto the top of the
strawberry.

FOR EASTER
Place some chocolate shavings over the ganache
(do this when the ganache is still wet) and top
with some Easter eggs. You can make chocolate
handles, AQ pls give instructions? if you like,
using melted chocolate in a piping bag, then set.

Ghost Pops Marshmallow

Makes 12

1 cup water

2½ tablespoons powdered gelatin

1½ cups caster (superfine) sugar

1 cup corn or glucose syrup

pinch salt

edible colour if desired

⅓ cup icing (confectioners') sugar
   plus extra for dusting

¼ cup cornflour (cornstarch)

300 g (10½ oz) white chocolate

12 popsticks

Place ½ cup lukewarm water into a shallow bowl. Sprinkle the gelatin powder over the surface of the water and allow to soften a few minutes.

Meanwhile in a saucepan, place ½ cup water, the sugar, the syrup and salt. On medium heat, cook for 4 minutes with a lid on. Remove the lid and cook a further 7–8 minutes until temperature reaches 115°C/240°F on a sugar thermometre. Allow to cool for a few minutes.

Place the gelatin mixture into the bowl of a stand mixer. Whisk on a low speed for 1 minute. Gradually add the sugar mixture in a slow steady drizzle, while beating, until all the mixture is incorporated. If you're adding colour, place 2–3 drops in now. Switch to high speed and beat for 12–15 minutes until thick and meringue like.

Grease and line a 3cm (1in) deep, 12 x 8cm (4 ¾ x 3in) baking tray with non-stick paper. Mix the icing sugar and cornflour and place one-third of it over the non-stick paper (bottom and sides). Spread the marshmallow mixture evenly into the lined pan and allow to set for several hours or overnight (do not refrigerate).

Sprinkle another third of the cornflour mixture liberally over the top of the marshmallow. Turn out the marshmallow onto a chopping board sprinkled with more cornflour mix. Use a round cookie cutter to cut 12 marshmallow cylinders. Toss these in the cornflour mix to coat and shake off excess powder.

Melt the white chocolate on medium heat in the microwave or over double boiler. Prepare a styrofoam block or similar.

Dip one end of each pop stick into a little white chocolate and insert one into each of the marshmallow cylinders. Place on to a tray and refrigerate for an hour until set. Re-melt the white chocolate and allow to cool a few minutes. Dip each marshmallow into the white chocolate. Let excess chocolate drip off and place popsticks into styrofoam block. Set in the fridge for a few hours and serve.

Sweet Potato Jack-o'-lanterns

Makes 30

2 large sweet potatoes, peeled
2 tablespoons olive oil

Preheat oven to 190°C/375°F/Gas mark 5. Line 2 baking trays with non-stick paper.

Cut a small 'V' from the top of the sweet potato along the length. Slice the sweet potatoes into 10-20 mm thick circles. Lay the circles flat with the cut section pointing up wards. Now, cut out two triangles for the eyes, one triangle for the nose and a mouth. Brush with a little oil on both sides and bake until golden–about 20–30 minutes.

Spider Cupcakes

Makes 18

1 cup double cream

1 portion vanilla cupcake batter

1 portion frosting or buttercream icing

500 g (17½ oz) dark chocolate, finely chopped

100 g (3½ oz) dark chocolate, melted

3 packet liquorice strips/strings

200 g (7 oz) white chocolate, melted

Cook a batch of cupcakes from this book and decorate with frosting.

Place the double cream in a saucepan over a medium heat. Place the chopped dark chocolate in a bowl. Bring the cream up to just boiling and turn off. Pour the cream over the chocolate and stir until smooth. Set aside and allow to cool to room temperature.

Using your hands, roll 18 balls 1½cm (2/3in) out of the chocolate. Place the balls onto a non-stick paper-lined tray. Use a skewer to make 4 holes in each side of the ball. Dip one end of the liquorice strips into the melted dark chocolate and feed it into the holes of the balls until you have 8 legs in each. Use the white chocolate in a piping bag to pipe out 2 eyes onto each of the spider bodies. Use remaining melted dark chocolate in a piping bag to make pupils for the eyes.

Allow to set, then transfer spiders to the tops of cupcakes and serve.

Eyeball Cordial

Makes 12

295g (10 oz) can sweetened
    condensed milk
16g (½ oz) powdered gelatin
cooking spray oil
food colouring pen
green, red and purple cordials

Lightly grease round ice cube trays.

Bring 1 cup of water to a boil in a saucepan. Stir in sweetened condensed milk then stir to incorporate.

In a small bowl with 1 cup of cold water sprinkle in 16g (½oz) of gelatin. Let stand about 1 minute to soften. Add ½ cup boiling water. Pour the unflavoured gelatin mixture into the milk mixture. Stir to combine.

Pour into round ice cube trays or alternatively pour into a slab/brownie tray, and refrigerate. Turn out jelly mixture when set. If you made it in a brownie tray, cut circles from the slab.

Decorate your eyeballs with a food colouring pen.

Make up different-coloured cordials and plop eyeballs in each cup.

Spider Webs

Makes 8-12

2 packets pretzel sticks (you can also
  use chocolate sticks)
300 g (10½ oz) white chocolate,
  melted
150 g (5 oz) dark chocolate, melted

Line 3 trays with non-stick baking paper. Place 2 pretzel sticks in a cross. Lay another two pretzels on top to form an 8-point star.

Place the white chocolate in a piping bag with a small plain nozzle. Starting in the middle, pipe a circle of white chocolate to hold the pretzels together, then carefully make a spiral of white chocolate until you reach the ends of the pretzel sticks, to make your spider web. Repeat for remaining spider webs. Allow to set for 30 minutes, then use the dark chocolate to pipe a spider in the centre. Allow to set for 15 minutes before serving

Easter Eggs

Makes 12

200 g (7 oz) white cooking
    chocolate
200 g (7 oz) milk cooking chocolate
½ cup thick double cream
2 easter egg mould sheets with 12
    shapes in each

Place half the white chocolate over a double boiler and stir gently until smooth. Reserve 2 tablespoons of the chocolate and set aside. Using a clean pastry brush, paint a thin layer of chocolate over one egg mould sheet. Do exactly the same with half the milk chocolate, setting aside 2 tablespoons. Paint the remaining sheet with the milk chocolate. Leave aside to set.

Meanwhile, place the remaining unmelted white chocolate together with half the cream over a double boiler and stir until smooth. Cover and set in the fridge for one hour until thickened. Repeat for the milk chocolate.

Spoon the mixtures into the egg moulds, smoothing the surface. Chill for 20 minutes. Turn out the 'eggs'. You will have 24 halves. Use the remaining melted chocolate (you may need to re-melt on low in the microwave), to join two halves to make an egg. Repeat for all and serve.

Basic
Recipes

Basic Recipes

You're already superheroes, juggling busy lives and families. You don't need to be running around trying to create professionally designed cakes or catering. In this book we've created easy recipe ideas that are achievable whether you're a novice or expert in the kitchen. Just remember to have fun and get the kids helping.

The cake recipes featured are all interchangeable, so you can choose your favourite flavour and decorate it according to the theme. We've chosen buttercream icing to cover most of the cakes as it's so easy to use, and requires no special tools as with fondant or marzipan designs, and kids enjoy eating it more than the hard sugar icing. If you are well versed in fondant covering and have the tools required, you can use this method to achieve a store-bought finish.

Most recipes don't need specialised equipment; however the few that do will have it listed in the ingredients list and an alternative is provided. A piping bag is the most you'll need for the majority of the recipes.

There are a few basic techniques listed below, to help out the beginners. We hope you enjoy making these as much as we did!

Working with fondant icing

Fondant icing is often used to cover sponge and fruit cakes. It provides a smooth even layer over the surface of the c-ke and presents a good surface on which to add decorations. It can also be used to mould decorative shapes for cake tops. Fondant can be tinted with colour and flavour. It can be made from scratch, but we prefer to buy it ready-made. Good-quality fondants are readily available from specialty cake shops.

Colouring fondant icing

Colour fondant icing with gel or powder colours, available from sugarcraft specialists, as they don't affect the consistency of the fondant. If you have liquid colours simply add some icing (confectioners') sugar with the liquid colour to keep the fondant from becoming too sticky. Add a dab of colour (you can add more later) to the centre of fondant. Fold the fondant over several times with your fingers until the colour is mixed in. Black and red are difficult to achieve a rich colour, so it is better to buy pre-coloured fondant. For brown fondant, you can use a little melted chocolate with icing sugar or cocoa to achieve a rich base colour to which you can add more colour.

To roll out fondant icing: For a smooth finish, use a glass bottle to roll out the icing as a wooden rolling pin can leave small imprints.

To stick fondant icing together: Fondant is mostly sugar so a little dab of water with your finger will act like glue by dissolving the sugar in the fondant.

To make fondant shine: Use the steam from your iron over your fondant art to create a shine. Fondant shine spray available.

Icings

ROYAL ICING

2 egg whites
10 ml (2 teaspoons) fresh lemon juice
370 g (13 oz) icing (confectioners') sugar

In a large bowl, whisk the egg whites with electric beaters until creamy. Sift in the icing sugar gradually, together with the lemon juice.

For piping, add more icing sugar to make a stiffer consistency. Colour with food colouring.

For icing a cake, use straightaway.

For 'flooding', colouring larger areas, add 5–10 ml (1–2 teaspoons) water at a time to a batch of Royal Icing until you have runnier icing. It will keep in the refrigerator, covered with a damp cloth to stop a skin forming, for up to a week.

CHOCOLATE GANACHE

This is a rich chocolate icing.

250 g (9 oz) plain (dark) chocolate*
80 ml (2½ fl oz) double (heavy) cream

Place chocolate in a heatproof bowl.

Warm the cream in a small pan on the stove and bring to just boiling. Remove from heat and pour over chocolate. Stir until smooth.

*Minimum 50 per cent cocoa solids works best for shine but if concerned with bitterness, you can use a lower percentage. I don't recommend using milk chocolate as it has a high oil content and may split the ganache.

BUTTERCREAM FROSTING

300 g (10 oz) butter, softened
500 g (17 oz) icing (confectioners') sugar
1½ tablespoons milk
10 ml (2 teaspoons) vanilla extract

In a large bowl, beat the butter and the icing sugar with an electric whisk until combined. Add the milk and vanilla and beat until creamy. Colour as desired.

Variations

For cream cheese: add 100 g (3½ oz) cream cheese and beat well.

For chocolate: Add 2 tablespoons cocoa or 50 g (1 ¾ oz) cooled melted chocolate

For passionfruit: Add 30 ml (2 tablespoons) passionfruit pulp.

For piping or writing: add an extra 50–100 g (1¾–3½ oz) of icing sugar to stiffen the icing. It'll be easier to work with and will set hard.

Special Notes

- Double boiler: Place some water into a saucepan and bring to a boil. Place a bowl over the saucepan ensuring the water does not touch the bottom of the bowl. Reduce to a simmer. Place chocolate in the bowl and leave to melt.
- We always use 24 cm (10 in) cake tins (pans) unless otherwise stated.
- Some recipes feature nuts, but they can be made without.
- A dairy-free option is available, which can be substituted for other cakes, and decorated with Royal Icing.

notes

Recipe Index

First published in 2013 by
New Holland Publishers
London • Sydney • Cape Town • Auckland
www.newhollandpublishers.com • www.newholland.com.au

Garfield House 86–88 Edgware Road London W2 2EA United Kingdom
1/66 Gibbes Street Chatswood NSW 2067 Australia
Wembley Square First Floor Solan Road Gardens Cape Town 8001 South Africa
218 Lake Road Northcote Auckland New Zealand

A catalogue record of this book is available at the British Library and at the National Library of Australia

ISBN: 9781742573700

10 9 8 7 6 5 4 3 2 1

Publisher: Lliane Clarke
Editor: Simona Hill
Project editor: Jodi De Vantier
Designer: Tracy Loughlin
Photographer: Andy Lewis
Production director: Olga Dementiev
Printer: Toppan Leefung Printing Limited

Follow New Holland Publishers on
Facebook: www.facebook.com/NewHollandPublishers